PARTY MIX

21 Creative Plans for
Fun Fellowship

PARTY MIX

KAROL K. LADD

BROADMAN
& HOLMAN
PUBLISHERS

Nashville, Tennessee

Published by
Broadman & Holman Publishers, Nashville, Tennessee
Acquisitions & Development Editor: Vicki Crumpton
Interior Design: Desktop Miracles, Addison, Texas
Printed in the United States of America

4260-95
0-8054-6095-0

Dewey Decimal Classification: 793.2
Subject Heading: FELLOWSHIP ACTIVITIES /
CHURCH RECREATION PARTIES
Library of Congress Card Catalog Number: 96-26872

Unless otherwise noted, Scripture quotations are from the New King James Version, copyright © 1979, 1980, 1982, Thomas Nelson, Inc., Publishers. Those marked NASB are from the New American Standard Bible, © the Lockman Foundation, 1960, 1962, 1963, 1968, 1971, 1972, 1973, 1975, 1977, used by permission; TLB, The Living Bible, copyright © Tyndale House Publishers, Wheaton, Ill., 1971, used by permission.

Library of Congress Cataloging-in-Publication Data
Ladd, Karol.
     Party mix : 21 creative plans for fun fellowship / Karol K. Ladd
        p.   cm.
     ISBN 0-8054-6095-0 (pbk.)
     1. Entertaining—Planning. 2. Games. 3. Recipes. I. Title.
GV1471.L26   1997
793.2—dc20
                                                                    96-26872
                                                                    CIP

99 00 01 5 4 3

In loving memory of my mother,

Barbara Kinder,

who was truly a gifted and gracious hostess.

CONTENTS

ACKNOWLEDGMENTS

Many thanks to the friends who gave their time and input for the preparations of this book: Carol Potts, Beth Dykhuizen, Leslie Hodge, Amy Reppert, Carol Bayless, Lisa Flag, Reeve Pearce, and Patti Beckett.

A special thanks to supersleuth Katy Glentzer for her contributions and ideas for the Mystery Party. Most of all, thank you to my precious family, Curt, Grace, and Joy for their constant encouragement and support of this exciting endeavor!

Introduction

Fellowship with friends is one of life's great pleasures! There is great refreshment and joy in spending quality time with those you hold dear. Creative parties certainly provide a catalyst for these memorable times. As you open the door of your home, you are opening up tremendous opportunities to not only encourage relationships, but also to share Christ's love and compassion with those around you. Who can know the countless lives that have been changed over a cup of tea, a dinner party, or a special celebration?

Most likely you will find yourself entertaining many times throughout the year. There are birthdays, weddings, graduations, and holidays that all require celebrations—not to mention the planned parties and fellowships with dinner clubs, neighborhood associations, circles, committees, Sunday school classes, and parent clubs. Do you sometimes feel overwhelmed when it comes to hosting an event? Perhaps you enjoy entertaining, but you could use a few new ideas for themes and events.

My goal is to help you entertain with ease and creativity, not anxiety. Hospitality should be simple, delightful, and fun for both the host and the guests! With your *Party Mix* resource book, you will have all of the tools you need to plan a party or social gathering from start to finish. These easy-to-do ideas are not only budget minded, but time conscious to fit even the busiest of schedules. Today's style of entertainment does not require long hours of preparation, using only gourmet recipes. Thankfully, relaxed settings with simple preparations are all that is needed to create wonderful times of fellowship among friends.

Even the most reluctant host or hostess can find confidence and encouragement through the suggestions in this book. While the first chapter provides practical hospitality tips, the chapters to follow are packed full of ideas for invitations, decorations, menus, and activities. Choose from nine theme parties in section 1, five event celebrations listed in section 2, or seven holiday gatherings found in section 3. "Conversation boosters" are included in most chapters to help you ignite dialogue between guests and possibly open up a hearty discussion.

A multitude of games and activities are also included in this book. Some people enjoy games while others do not, so you will need to evaluate your group and the purpose of the event. If your guests are more reserved, then skip the games and use only the conversation booster during the evening. There are many who enjoy activities that build interaction and help guests to get to know one another. Pick and choose the activities and themes that suit your group and your entertainment style.

Every chapter has many ideas for food, decorations, and activities. You can select what you want to do according to your budget and your schedule. Some people may go the extra mile with decorations, place settings, food, and games. This is nice but, as I said earlier, not necessary. The success of the event does not depend on carrying out every single suggestion listed in each chapter. The true success of the event depends on the gracious and relaxed attitude of the host or hostess!

At the beginning of some chapters, you will find special labels. The "Low Maintenance" label signals especially quick and easy events. Although this book provides many time-conscious ideas, the Low Maintenance parties are especially easy and can be pulled together at short notice or in between a hectic schedule. I have also labeled several parties as "Family Friendly." These are social gatherings that will work well as both "all adult" parties or "children included" events. How rewarding to have parties that create opportunities for family bonding as well as wonderful fellowship with others!

Do you love to cook? You'll be glad to discover complete menus filled with delicious recipes within the party themes. I prefer "real people" recipes that taste great, but are not a tremendous hassle to put together. Family, friends, and a variety of sources have contributed to the collection of recipes within these pages. Most certainly, these time-honored, taste-tested delights will bring a smile to even the most discerning of guests. If you prefer not to cook, you can always plan a potluck or purchase ready-made party platters or consider having the event catered.

One of the purposes of this book is to provide you with a source for "good clean fun." The creative and meaningful entertainment themes can be enjoyed by church groups, family members, neighbors, and friends of all ages. Several years ago I began to feel a void in Christian hospitality when I attended a Mystery Party—the fifth one that I had been to. Each party was slightly different, but basically each guest was required to role-play a very confusing and usually immoral individual. I had enough of the secular versions and decided it was time to put together creative adult party ideas that bring glory to God. You'll find the Usolvit Mystery Dinner Party in chapter 9.

After talking to a Christian bookstore owner, I also discovered that customers were constantly looking for shower and event party ideas, so this became another important aspect of the book. And of course, who can overlook the holidays with so many opportunities to open our homes to visitors? Most of these event and holiday parties can be used as opportunities to share Christ either through discussion or activities. Helpful ideas are included in each chapter.

Are you waiting for the perfect house before you entertain? Are you going to start entertaining when you have a little more free time? Perhaps you are waiting for a new dining room table or a matching set of dishes. Let's face it, the house will never be exactly perfect, and you will never have a little more free time. The time is now to jump right into hospitality!

Take a look at your calendar and begin planning that next dinner party with your friends. You have all the help you need in this handy resource book!

Keep in mind that much of Jesus' ministry took place over the dinner table, from the wedding at Cana to Zacchaeus' dinner table to the Last Supper. The hospitality of many gracious hosts and hostesses allowed an open door to Christ's ministry. No matter what resources or talents you possess, God can take your willingness and obedience and use it in ways far beyond your imagination. I am reminded of my neighbor Sylvia, who ministers to others through serving tea in her home on any given afternoon. Or Beth (mother of four), who always has a little extra food in the pot for anyone who happens to stop by for a visit. Or our Sunday school teacher, Jim, who can throw together a potluck quicker than you can say, "sign-up sheet." People such as these truly know and practice hospitality.

Paul told the early Christians to be "given to hospitality" (Rom. 12:13). Literally he meant for us to pursue it. We must be deliberate about entertaining others or it just won't happen. Keep in mind that there are few activities more rewarding in life than providing delightful and enjoyable gatherings for friends, family, and acquaintances. May you continually experience the joy of hospitality!

Chapter 1

HELPFUL HINTS ON HOW TO HOST

What is the key to successful hospitality? Is it exquisite food served with perfect place settings in the midst of incredibly lavish decor? Not at all! Hospitality is from the heart. Certainly food and presentation are important, but the foundation to successful entertainment rests in the relaxed and enjoyable atmosphere created by the host or hostess. Think back to a memorable evening that you have experienced in someone else's home. Was it the perfectly clean floor or the lovely dishes or the unique salad that made the evening special? Or would you say that your fondest memory is that of being with delightful people and experiencing meaningful conversations in a comfortable setting? The focus of *Party Mix* is not on being a "perfect" host or hostess, but being a gracious one, showing consideration for the needs of the guests.

As you plan your party, certain questions arise, such as: What is the best time for a party? Whom do I invite? How do I know where to seat my guests? How do I greet at the door, and how do I say good-bye? Should I provide a sit-down dinner or serve buffet-style? Do I need to play games or have activities for adults? For easy reference you will find the answers to these questions under five separate headings in this chapter. The sections are listed in progressive order as you would plan a party from start to finish.

- Purpose and Planning: Party themes and goals
- People: Guest lists, personalities
- Preparation: Organizing the event from invitations to recipes to schedule of activities
- Presentation: Table settings, napkins, and food presentation
- Party Etiquette: Greeting, seating, and eating with finesse

Purpose and Planning

Behind every great endeavor is a worthwhile purpose. What goal do you have in mind for your party? Is it to build relationships that have already been established or is it to create new relationships? Is this party related to an event or a holiday? Or is it just for fun? Build the event around your purpose.

You will discover many reasons to get together with others throughout the entire year. A Sunday school class fellowship, a new neighbor on the block, or just wanting to catch up with old friends. Choose the type of party that fits your needs and interests. Here is a general chart to assist you in coordinating the type of party with the purpose. Party titles listed here are fully explained throughout the book.

PEOPLE	PURPOSE	PLAN
Large group: 20 or more guests (church fellowships, neighborhood socials, work-related parties, reunions). Generally consists of acquaintances, a few good friends, and perhaps some people you do not know at all.	To introduce and build relationships.	Potlucks, theme parties such as Western, Mexican, Hawaiian, Back to School, Dessert Party, or Picnic. More mingling, fewer games (perhaps none).

PEOPLE	PURPOSE	PLAN
Medium-sized group: 8–20 guests (Sunday School class, office parties, get-togethers with friends). Generally consists of good friends and acquaintances.	To deepen and enhance relationships and enjoy fun and fellowship together.	Mystery Party, Cook by the Book, Sea Cruise, Video Adventure, holiday parties, progressive dinners, event and theme parties.
Small group: 4–8 guests (Small fellowship or Bible study groups, neighbors). Generally consists of couples, co-workers, close friends and companions.	To get to know people better and spend quality time together.	Dessert Party, Valentines Dinner, holiday parties, Formal Dinner Party, any theme party or event. Games are more appropriate.

People

How do you know whom to invite to your parties? For many events, the decisions are made for you. If you are giving a shower, a birthday party, or an honorary event of any type, the guest list is provided by the honoree. If you are planning a fellowship for Sunday school or church, then every person on the roll should be included. When you are planning your own event and the guest list is up to you, there are several points of consideration.

First, how many people are you able to serve at one time? Consider the size of your home, the table space, and grocery budget. Do not feel that you must pay back every social obligation at one time. More parties with fewer people may be your best option.

Create a good blend of guests. Invite people with a wide range of interests who perhaps have a little something in common. These shared interests help to build a basis for better conversation.

Consider the various personalities of your guests. If they are a fun-loving bunch, then they will probably enjoy events such as the Video Scavenger Hunt or dress-up themes. Others may enjoy trivia or word games, so invite people of this nature to a mystery party, dessert or dinner party with thinking games included. If you intend to invite a more reserved group of people, then eliminate games altogether and enjoy a lovely (possibly theme-related) dinner party. Assess the likes and dislikes of your guests and decide accordingly.

Should you invite children? This depends on the type of event you are planning and your personal comfort level. Events such as picnics, western parties, and certain celebrations are family-friendly (and are labeled so in this book). Also ask yourself: Can the couple I am inviting afford a sitter? Do they have a nursing baby? Are their children holy terrors? If you would rather children not be included in the event, then ask the invited guest, "Do you think you can get a baby-sitter for Saturday night?"

What do you do with your own children if you are entertaining only adults? You may consider a baby-sitter who will keep the kids in another part of the house during the event or allow them to visit a relative or friend for the evening. If they are older children and well mannered, then certainly include them in the event. It is good to try to include your children as often as possible, helping them to practice good social skills and manners.

One final note concerning the people that you invite to your home: the word *hospitality* in the Bible actually refers to a love for strangers. The Greek word for hospitality, *philoxenia,* breaks down to *philos,* meaning brotherly love, and *xenos,* which is the word for strangers. Jesus referred to this very thing in Luke 14:12–14: "When you put on a dinner," he said, "don't invite friends, brothers, relatives, and rich neighbors! For they will return the invitation. Instead, invite the poor, the crippled, the lame, and the blind. Then at the resurrection of the godly, God will reward you for inviting those who can't repay you" (TLB).

As you make your invitation list, I encourage you to be open to visitors at church or new neighbors. Include people that you do not know very well. New friendships may be formed, and both the host and the guests will be blessed.

Preparation

With proper planning and preparation before the party, you can remain relaxed during the event. Your preparation includes four basic areas: invitations, decorations, food, and activities. The decisions you make on what to do in these areas are based on your budget and the time that you have available to prepare for the party. Although each chapter is full of ideas for specific parties, you do not need to use all of the ideas. Pick those that fit your schedule, your guests, and your spending allowance.

Make your lists and check them twice. As you begin your party planning, you will actually need several lists. Prepare a menu list that identifies all of the foods you would like to serve. Be sure to keep this list on hand for the day of the party. Have you ever thrown a party and after it was over, looked in the refrigerator to find a plate of hors d'oeuvres that you forgot to set out for the guests? I have!

You will also need several shopping lists, not only for food, but for decorations and activity supplies. Another list covers a schedule of events during the party that should be loosely followed. The final list is the preparation schedule for planning your time to make the food and other items before the party. Pace yourself so that you are not overloaded with too much on the day of the party.

Invitations
Generally your invitations should be prepared three weeks before the event and mailed within two to two and a half weeks of the party (a formal dinner or reception invitation should be

issued three weeks in advance). Once the invitations are in the mail, begin purchasing and preparing decorations and game items. One week before the party, purchase food for the event and begin simple but progressive food preparations. If you are having the event catered, then make your contacts three weeks to a month in advance. Check with the caterer one week prior, and the day before the event for any last-minute changes.

Invitations can be extended by phone or mail. For formal dinners or events, a written invitation is preferable. If you are hostessing an informal party or family gathering, then you may choose either route. A written invitation is helpful because it serves as a visual reminder of the event. Every party in this book includes an invitation suggestion. Include a map in the invitation if you are inviting guests that are unfamiliar with where you live. This will prevent last-minute phone calls asking for directions while you are getting ready for the party.

State on the invitation the type of party and who should be coming to it. For instance, if it is a couple's shower, write "couple's shower" on the invitation. Do not assume the guests will simply notice it is addressed to both husband and wife on the envelope. It is also helpful to tell if children are included or not (see People section in this chapter).

For most parties it is best to have a general head count of guests in order to know how much food to prepare. Add RSVP ("respond if you please") with your phone number to your invitation. It is also helpful to indicate the attire for the evening. What do all of the terms really mean? Here is a brief review:

"Black tie" or "Formal" means a tuxedo for men; women wear a cocktail or evening gown. "Semiformal" typically means that women wear dresses or good slacks and men wear sports shirts and slacks. In certain areas of the country, "semi-formal" means dresses for women and suits with ties for men. If in doubt, check it out. "Informal" or "Casual" refers to comfortable, yet neat, clothing that fits the occasion. For an outdoor picnic it would mean shorts and a shirt.

Decorations and Atmosphere

Decorations for an event should fit your own personality. Some people enjoy creative and theme-related decorations. These certainly add to the ambiance of the event, but decorations are not vital for an adult party. If you do not feel comfortable "playing up" a theme or holiday, then don't. Be yourself and let your decorations reflect the real you. Decorations also do not need to be costly. Many times you can use what you already have around the house.

Enhance your floral arrangements to fit the theme by adding ribbons, bows, or small items. Books can add to your decor. For a mystery party, place spy novels on coffee tables and buffet tables. For a tropical party, use travel brochures or books about the area. A bargain bookstore can produce many treasures. Books used as decorative items can also be given away as gifts.

Background music is another way to decorate your home for the event. Before a party, I always try to think of appropriate music that will carry out the theme. Resale shops are a wonderful source of current and older tunes. Just as decorations appeal to the eyes and the ears, they also appeal to our sense of smell. The scent of potpourri or scented candles can be a lovely addition to the atmosphere of the event.

Door decorations not only assure your guests that they have found the correct address, but they also act as a sign of welcome that builds intrigue to the event. A theme or holiday wreath or a creative welcome sign are simple, yet important, aspects of your decorating. Specific ideas are included with each chapter. Balloons are not necessary for an adult party, but they do add to the festivity of certain events. Use them outside tied in bunches or made into an arch. You may choose to use them inside, hanging free from the ceiling or tied to chairs and other objects.

Heavier cleaning should take place several days before the party, so that on the day of the event all you need to do is wipe down counters and mirrors and pick up clutter. For those of you who are housecleaning perfectionists, remember that a house does not need to be immaculate before you entertain. It is more important to present a welcome and relaxed environment than a sterile one.

Food
One week before the party, plan your menu and carefully prepare a shopping list. Determine which items you can prepare ahead of time and begin preparing one or two items each day up until the party. You will find that this keeps you at ease on the day of the party and helps you keep your kitchen in order as well.

Activities
Game and activity preparations are usually simple. Decide before the party what activities you think may fit the personality of your guests and prepare accordingly. If your guests are the type that would like to get to know one another better, then plan an icebreaker activity at the beginning of the party. It is good to have a few games up your sleeve (prepared and ready to play) if you sense that the atmosphere and mixture of guests is right. If you choose not to do the games, that's fine, save them for the next party. Many guests enjoy simply eating and talking.

Most chapters in this book provide "conversation boosters" in addition to the suggested activities. You may want to only use the conversation booster and not planned games or activities. It is your job as a host or hostess to decide if the momentum is right for games. If in doubt, privately get the opinion of several other guests who are good friends. I've found that most people enjoy games once they get going, even if they are hesitant at first.

As you prepare the party-day schedule, be sure to pencil in time to relax and pray before the party. Perhaps a short nap, a nice warm bath, or a quiet moment with a good book will relax you. Pace yourself during the day to provide enough time. Prayer is a vital part of your preparation as well. Pray for a loving and gracious spirit during the event, pray for your guests, and pray for the smoothness of the party and activities. Keep in mind Philippians 4:6–7 (TLB): "Don't worry about anything; instead, pray about everything; tell God your needs and don't forget to thank him for his answers. If you do this you will experience God's peace, which is far more wonderful than the human mind can understand. His peace will keep your thoughts and your hearts quiet and at rest as you trust in Christ Jesus."

Presentation

The presentation of your home and your food does not need to be elaborate and expensive to be elegant and inviting. Simple touches can add so much to the overall effect of the party. One important presentation decision is whether to serve dinner as a sit-down affair or buffet-style service. You can serve more guests if you entertain buffet-style; so if you are planning for a larger group (10 or more), the buffet may be your best option.

Buffet Presentation
Arrange food and utensils in an attractive manner so that guests can help themselves easily and conveniently. (It is helpful to roll the needed utensils in napkins and tie the bundles with theme-related ribbons for each guest.) Combine buffet service with sit-down dining by providing small eating tables. Trays are another option if you are serving heavier foods. For finger foods, hand-held plates are fine.

The Table Setting
For a more formal occasion with fewer guests, you may choose to have a sit-down dinner at tables set in traditional style. Folded napkins and napkin rings are special ways to add to your table presentation.

Although there are entire books on this subject, here is one simple folded napkin idea that will work for many occasions.

FAN-FOLDED NAPKINS

Spread napkin out in front of you with the wrong side up. Fold in half taking the lower edge up at the middle. Fold in half again and turn the napkin 90 degrees. Starting at the short side, fold the rectangle in small one-inch folds back and forth, accordion-style. Press folded napkin together. Hold lower edge in one hand and pull upper edges to the left and right respectively to create the fan. Carefully place the napkin at the dinner setting either in a cup or napkin ring, keeping it in a fan-like position.

Centerpieces add to the appearance of your tables, whether buffet or sit-down. You will find that each party in this book has its own suggestions, and keep in mind that floral arrangements, candles, or baskets can be made to fit any theme. Remember to keep your centerpiece low so that people can see over it and maintain conversation across the table.

Place cards are helpful in eliminating the mystery or awkwardness as to where each guest will sit. Generally at official dinner parties the courtesy title and surname are written on the place card, such as Dr. Thomas or Mrs. Brown. At a less formal gathering with friends and relatives, both first and last names are used.

Concerning table settings, basic traditions still apply although recent emphasis on more informal and innovative entertaining has loosened the rules slightly. Usually, plates are set about one inch from the edge of the table. Bread and butter plates are placed to the left of the dinner plate, above the forks and parallel to the glasses. When salad is served with dinner (as is often done in informal entertaining), the salad plate can replace the bread and butter plate and be used for both salad and bread.

Water and tea glasses are generally placed above the knife to the right of the plate. Water can be poured before the guests are seated. The water glass is placed closest to the dinner plate. Cups and saucers intended for after-dinner coffee or tea may be present on the table during dinner or added at serving time. They are usually placed to the right of the water and tea glasses.

Flatware is placed so that the bottom edge is aligned with the dinner plate. Knives go to the right of the plate (with cutting edge facing in). Bread and butter spreaders are placed across the bread and butter plate. Spoons are placed to the right of the knife. Salad and dinner forks are placed to the left of the dinner plate while dessert forks can be placed (along with coffee spoon) horizontally at the top of the plate. Seafood forks are the only exception to the rule and are placed on the far right of the spoons. Utensils should be placed in the order in which they will be used during the meal.

The Food Presentation

Attractive food presentations can be made easily with just a few simple additions. Variety is key. Your food menu should have a wide diversity of color, texture, and ingredients, whether on the plate or in buffet serving dishes. Sprigs of parsley, orange or lemon slices, a drizzle of butter, or even a fresh flower can make a so-so presentation into an elegant one.

Party Etiquette

Greeting

One of the most important aspects of hosting an event is greeting your guests at the door. This makes your guests feel comfortable and sets the tone for the evening. Always greet with a smile and a kind salutation, such as "Welcome. I'm glad you could come." How do you greet at the door if you are preparing the food in the kitchen? There are basically two solutions:

1. Prepare your food ahead of time so that you can be available at the door for greeting. This takes careful planning. You can always take a break from the kitchen as guests arrive and then return to the kitchen for final preparations as your guests mingle. Make sure that your guests have something to drink and eat while you are busy in the kitchen.

2. Allow a co-host or other guest to help as the greeter or in the kitchen. If you have a cohost, the greeting and food responsibility should be shared and decided upon before the party. If you do not have a cohost, ask a close friend to arrive a little early and help you. Another idea is to play greeter tag. Greet the first guest at the door and inform him that he is the new greeter. The next person to arrive will become the next greeter and so on. This is a wonderful way to create mingling and allow guests to get to know one another while you are handling food preparations.

Seating

Generally if you have an even number of guests, the hostess sits at one end of the table (nearest the kitchen) and the host sits at the opposite end. If the hostess does not have a host, she may ask a friend to act as a host. Guests sit in between the hosts, alternating men and women. Male and female guests of honor sit to the right of the hostess and host respectively. If the balance of male and female is not even between the host and hostess, then the hostess generally moves one seat to the left, allowing the man of honor to sit at the end.

In designating a seating arrangement, it is wise to seat talkers next to listeners. Also, try to seat people near each other who are compatible with one another and share common interests. A dinner party is not the best time to try to patch rifts between people by seating them next to one another.

Serving

Dishes are always presented at the left of the person being served and removed from the right. It is helpful to remember RR: removed at the right. In certain situations it is permissible to remove from the left, as in the case of a glass or a knife that could only otherwise be removed by reaching across your guest.

Serving dishes should be passed counterclockwise, from left to right around the table. Hot food should be served while it is still mildly hot. There is nothing worse than serving cold food that is supposed to be hot. As the hostess, it is your responsibility to tell the guests to begin eating even though you may still be serving one or two more guests.

Leaving

How long should a party last? Showers, teas, and event parties generally will last one and a half to two hours. Picnics and other parties are longer due to content. Open houses should be scheduled for three-hour periods and are commonly known as come-and-go events. Be sure to add an ending time to the invitation, unless you want to keep it open ended.

How do you let people know that the party is over? Unless you have other obligations or are extremely tired and desire that your guests leave, allow them to stay past the ending time of the party and enjoy a relaxing time together. Some guests may ask to stay longer to help clean up. This should be considered a welcomed help and rarely denied, as it can lead to a delightful time of visiting in the kitchen after most guests have left.

Miss Manners, in her guidebook to "excruciatingly correct behavior," suggests that if you are ready for your guests to depart, then you as the host can merely stand up, graciously smile, and say, "I'm so glad you joined us this evening."[1] I want to emphasize that this is a last resort and should rarely if ever be used. I am amused at the story that Emily Post tells of the kindly professor and host who looked at his wife and said, "Well my dear, don't you think it is time we went to bed so these good people can go home?"[2]

At some theme parties, you may want to give a small gift or bag of goodies as a reminder of the evening, although you certainly do not need to do so. (On the other hand, presenting goody bags may be a helpful, nonverbal signal that the party is over!) When it comes to visiting another home for dinner or a party, do not feel obligated to bring a gift to the hostess. It is courteous to ask the hostess if you can bring a dish of food to contribute to the dinner.

It is not wise to surprise the hostess with a food or dessert item, as this may offset the balance of her preplanned menu. If you truly want to bring a gift and the hostess insists that you do not help with the food, then fresh flowers or a small plant are in order. If a party is given in your honor, then you should consider sending flowers to the hostess before the event.

Final Note

Whether you are encouraging fellowship with other believers or developing relationships with nonbelievers, hospitality is a part of God's work. Your home can be an open door to show Christ's love and to offer encouragement to others. Jesus Himself took time to fellowship—sometimes in small homes, sometimes in large gatherings, sometimes with believers, sometimes with strangers and nonbelievers. Use the resources He has given you, great or small, to entertain others and build relationships for His glory!

---

1. Judith Martin, *Miss Manners* (New York, N.Y.: Warner Books, 1982), 468.

2. Elizabeth L. Post, *Emily Post on Entertaining* (New York, N.Y.: HarperCollins Publishers, 1994) 15.

THEME PARTIES

My heart overflows with a good theme.

PSALM 45:1, NASB

Chapter 2

SENSATIONAL
SEA CRUISE

CRUISE SCHEDULE • 2 HOURS

30 minutes:	Arrival, mingle, The World's Largest Photo Album, The Worldwide Travel Mixer, appetizers
40 minutes:	Seafood Buffet
50 minutes:	Dessert and Terrific Travel Trivia Game

APPROXIMATE CRUISE CAPACITY • 5–25

Sail away aboard a wonderful sea cruise in the comfort of your own home. Your guests will enjoy a delicious seafood buffet while sharing highlights from their own favorite vacations. After dinner, play the original and fantastically fun Sea Cruise Trivia game. In this chapter you'll find all the help you need for a successful and exciting cruise. Bon Voyage!

Travel Ticket Invitations

Create unique invitations that resemble a cruise ticket. Use colored paper (8½ x 11) for the slip cover of the ticket. Fold into thirds and write on the outer flap, _____ Cruise Lines, putting your last name in the blank. Decorate the cover with beach or paradise stickers found at most craft stores. Inside, place a white ticket made from thick paper or thin cardboard. Type the following information for the ticket.

THIS TICKET ENTITLES BEARER TO ONE FANTASTIC TIME AT

A SENSATIONAL SEA CRUISE PARTY

Date of Departure: _____

Boarding Time:_____

Dock Location: _____

Stipulations:

Must bring several photos from favorite vacation.
Tourist Attire Required

Respond to Captain _____

Phone: _____

Use a business-size envelope to mail the invitation and don't forget to write "Tickets Enclosed" next to the guest's name and address on the envelope.

Seaworthy Decorations

Your best resource for decorations will be a local travel agency. Ask them if they would be willing to give away some of their extra posters or brochures to use for decorations at the party. Usually, travel agencies are more than willing to get rid of their old materials.

As with any party, your entrance decorations set the mood for the theme. You have several options. A travel poster hung on the door at a slight angle with a sign that reads, "Bon Voyage!" would make an intriguing welcome. Another idea for the front door is to attach a ring-shaped life preserver (found at pool supply stores or make your own using Styrofoam covered with white tape and a few ropes).

If you choose to go the extra mile, you may want to create the illusion of boarding a ship. On the path approaching your front door place chain railings to look like the entrance ramp of a cruise ship. This can be done without too much effort by using six to eight coffee cans covered with white paper. Fill them with sand or white rocks and place a white painted yardstick in each can. This will make the poles for your chain railings. Use plastic chains (found at most discount stores), thick ribbon, or white rope strung from the top of each stick.

Inside, decorate the walls using travel posters. Create a festive cruise ship atmosphere by using colorful helium balloons, flowers, and/or crepe paper streamers.

Food tables can be adorned with tourist paraphernalia. Items such as cameras, small travel bags, various state and national flags, travel brochures, sun glasses, passports, suntan lotion, packs of gum, and visors can create a great grouping for the centerpiece at each table. Add colorful confetti and a plastic lei at each place setting and you have a wonderful travel table setting. Luggage tags with each of the guest's names on them make perfect place cards. You can make your own luggage tags by cutting colored paper in a rectangular shape and covering the paper with clear contact or laminating paper. Attach yarn or plastic string to one edge of the card as the holder.

Most travel or video stores and agencies offer travel videos for rental. You may be able to find a cruise video or a video about the Caribbean or South Seas. Play the video silently as your guests arrive and mingle. Background music should be of a tropical, maritime, or sailing theme. Potpourri or candle scents could be sea breeze or tropical floral.

Arrival Activities

World's Largest Photo Album
As guests arrive greet them at the door with a grand welcome from the captain of the ship. The host and/or hostess should dress in white shirt, shorts, socks, and tennis shoes. You may even want to add some striped ribbons to the shoulders of your shirt.

Ask one friend to act as the photographer, taking pictures of the guests with the captain as they board the ship. Polaroid pictures would be perfect.

Give each guest a name tag with (<u>your last name</u>) Cruise Lines printed on the top. On a nearby table lay out several colored poster boards with the words, "My Favorite Vacation" written at the top. Since you have asked in the invitation for each person to bring their favorite vacation picture, allow them to place their picture on the poster board to help create The World's Largest Photo Album. Use white tacky substance to stick the pictures to the poster so that photos can be returned at the end of the party. Provide pens for people to write captions under their pictures. If you have a fun-loving group, they may want to add humorous (but tasteful) captions to other pictures as well.

The Worldwide Travel Mixer

After most of the guests have arrived, provide a Worldwide Travel questionnaire and pencil for each guest at the party. There are only five questions on the questionnaire, yet a great amount of interaction must take place in order to find the correct answers to the questions. The guests are to write the person's name who fits the description in the blank.

WORLDWIDE TRAVEL QUESTIONNAIRE

Find the person at this party who:

1. Has traveled to the *greatest* number of foreign countries._____

2. Has traveled to the *farthest* destination around the world from here. _____

3. Has spent the *longest* time on a cruise ship.

   _____

4. Has lost the *most* luggage on a trip.

   _____

5. Has had the *shortest* stay in any foreign country.

   _____

After about fifteen minutes, gather your guests together to evaluate their answers. You will find that there will be a variety of answers, so check the facts and see who is the true winner. Offer small gifts, such as a mini photo album or travel log, for prizes. This is a great game to help your guests get to know one another's names and a little about their life experiences.

Appetizers

Bon Voyage Punch

This punch is a refreshing delight. Make several batches.
It will go quickly!

2 pints cranberry juice cocktail 2 cups orange juice
¼ cup freshly squeezed lemon juice
1 quart pineapple sherbet   1 quart ginger ale

❖ Combine cranberry juice, orange juice, and lemon juice; beat in pineapple sherbet; then chill. Slowly pour in ginger ale just before serving. Add ice and serve immediately.
❖ Yields 12–15 punch cup servings

Three-Layer Crab Dip

2 (8 oz) pkg cream cheese, softened
½ cup mayonnaise   1 tsp white pepper
1 tsp Worcestershire sauce   ½ onion, grated
½ tsp minced garlic   picante sauce or salsa
1 can crabmeat, drained

❖ First layer: Blend first six ingredients and place in bottom of a shallow serving dish. Second layer: Cover with picante sauce. Third Layer: Top with crabmeat. Press evenly with fork or spatula, cover and refrigerate overnight. Serve with a variety of crackers.

Seafood Buffet Menu

Fruit and Salad
Shrimp Gumbo
Light and Crunchy Salmon Patties
Heavenly Sole

Rice Medley
Sweet Glazed Carrots
Hot Dinner Bread
Pineapple Upside-Down Cake
Chocolate Wonder

Most cruise lines are known for their spectacular buffets! With smart planning and very little effort, your presentation can be just as spectacular. Begin with the fruit and salad section including:

- Vegetable sticks and dip
- Fresh fruit (strawberries, grapes, pineapple, and watermelon chunks) served in a carved out watermelon
- Cheese cubes and crackers
- Tossed salad with a variety of toppings and dressings

Shrimp Gumbo

½ cup flour	bacon drippings
1 lb cooked and peeled shrimp	
1 cup chopped celery	1 bell pepper, chopped
2 onions, chopped	2 cloves garlic, minced
1 quart stewed tomatoes, pureed in blender	
1 large can okra	2 tsp filé
salt and pepper to taste	

❖ Brown flour in drippings. Add shrimp, celery, onion, garlic, and pepper. Cook until wilted. Add tomatoes and okra. Simmer 30 minutes. Remove from heat, add filé. Serve over rice.

❖ Yields 6–8 bowls.

For the main course of the buffet try:

Light and Crunchy Salmon Patties

1 (15 oz) can pink salmon	1 egg
⅓ cup minced onion	½ cup flour
1½ tsp baking powder	corn meal

❖ Drain salmon; put aside 2 Tbsp of the juice. Mix salmon, egg, and onion until sticky. Stir in flour. Add baking powder to salmon juice; stir into salmon mixture. Form into small patties and roll in corn meal. Fry until golden brown.

❖ Yields 6 patties.

Heavenly Sole

6 fresh or frozen sole, flounder, or orange roughy fillets
¼ cup margarine
¼ cup chopped onion
1 (16 oz) can diced tomatoes
1 (3 oz) can chopped mushrooms, drained
1 clove garlic, minced
1 Tbsp Italian seasonings

❖ Thaw fish, if frozen. Dot each fillet with 2 tsps of margarine; sprinkle with Italian seasonings. Roll up fillets; fasten with wooden toothpicks, if necessary. Place rolls in 10-inch skillet. Add undrained tomatoes, mushrooms, onion, and garlic. Cover and simmer 15 minutes or until fish flakes easily when tested with a fork. Remove fish to warm platter; keep hot.

❖ Cook tomato mixture, uncovered, over high heat 10 minutes or until thick. Spoon over fish. Garnish with lemon wedges.

❖ Yields 6 servings.

Rice Medley

2 scallions, chopped
1 Tbsp margarine, melted
1 (6 oz) pkg long grain and wild rice mix
2 cups chicken broth
1 (6 oz) pkg snow pea pods, thawed and drained
1 (4 oz) can water chestnuts, drained and sliced
2 Tbsp vegetable oil

❖ In a large skillet sauté scallions in margarine. Add rice mix and chicken broth and bring to a boil. Cover and reduce heat, simmer for 20-25 minutes.

❖ Sauté pea pods and water chestnuts in hot oil for 1–2 minutes. Combine rice and vegetables tossing gently.

❖ Yields 6–8 servings.

Sweet Glazed Carrots

1 lb fresh mini carrots	2 Tbsp margarine
2 Tbsp honey	

❖ Steam carrots until tender (about 3–5 minutes). In a large skillet melt margarine and slowly stir in honey. Add carrots and cook over low heat until carrots are well glazed.
❖ Yields 6-8 servings.

Hot Dinner Bread

1 loaf French or Italian bread

1 tsp parsley	¼ tsp dill weed
½ cup butter, softened	¼ tsp oregano, crumbled
1 clove garlic, minced	grated Parmesan cheese

❖ Blend butter, parsley, oregano, dill, and garlic. Slice bread and spread slices with butter mixture. Wrap loaf in foil, leaving the top open. Sprinkle the top with cheese and parsley flakes. Heat at 400° for 10 minutes.
❖ Yields 10–12 slices.

Conversation Booster

As an optional conversation starter during dinner, ask your guests to share with others sitting around them highlights from their favorite vacation or the funniest thing that ever happened to them on vacation.

After Dinner Fellowship

Dessert

After everyone has had enough time to eat and chat, invite your guests to enjoy some dessert and coffee during the trivia game.

Pineapple Upside Down Cake

2 Tbsp butter or margarine	½ cup brown sugar (packed)
4 pineapple rings, drained, reserving juice	
6 maraschino cherries, cut in fourths	
1¼ cups sifted enriched flour	½ cup sugar
2 tsp baking powder	½ tsp salt
⅓ cup shortening, softened	

½ cup minus 1 Tbsp pineapple juice
½ tsp grated lemon peel   1 egg

❖ Melt butter and pour into 8 x 8 pan. Evenly spread the brown sugar over the butter. Cut pineapple slices in half and arrange over the brown sugar butter mixture. Center each pineapple ring with three maraschino cherry pieces. Sift dry ingredients together over shortening. Add remaining ingredients and beat for two minutes. Pour batter over pineapple rings. Bake in moderate oven (350°) for 40 minutes. Let stand for 5 minutes and then turn upside down on large plate and serve.

❖ Yields 12–16 servings.

Chocolate Wonder

1 (7-ounce) chocolate-almond candy bar
18 large marshmallows   ½ cup milk
1 cup whipping cream, whipped
1 baked 9-inch pastry shell

❖ Combine candy, marshmallows, and milk in a heavy saucepan. Cover and cook over low heat until melted, stirring occasionally. Remove from heat; cool. Fold in whipped cream. Pour mixture into pastry shell. Chill at least 8 hours.

❖ Yields 8–10 slices.

Sea Cruise Trivia Game

Divide into two teams. You may want to divide men against women or divide by birthdays (those born January through June on one team and those born July through December on the other team). It is not vital that each team be exactly even in number, but you may want to shift around some of the team members if the teams are largely imbalanced. Give the teams one minute to come up with a name for their team.

The game is played by reading a question to one team. They may talk among themselves to come up with the answer within one minute. A spokesperson from the team is to give the team's answer. If the team gets the answer correct, they receive ten points. If they do not get the answer correct, the question goes to the other team who will try to answer it for five points. After both teams have had a chance to answer the question and neither team has answered correctly, then the question is dead and you move on to the next question.

Instead of the point system, you may choose to have a map of the world hanging in the room. Use two colored markers, one for each team. When a team answers correctly, mark one longitudinal line and progressively move from west to east. The first ship to reach the far east side of the map wins.

The questions are presented in categories. You may ask each team before they play to tell the category that they prefer.

The correct answer for each question is italicized.

GAME QUESTIONS

Category 1: The History of Luxury Liners[1]
1. The *Ile de France* (finished in 1927) is recognized as the first . . .
   a. cruise vessel to circle the world.
   b. French cruise ship on which every passenger became ill.
   c. *Floating luxury hotel or luxury liner.*

2. During World War II many luxury liners . . .
   a. stopped operations completely and took a tremendous loss.
   b. *were camouflaged and used for service as troop carriers.*
   c. were docked and used as military hiding places for heavy artillery.

3. In which decade of the twentieth century did charter sailing and pleasure cruises become a popular and frequent activity?
   a. 10s
   b. *20s*
   c. 30s

4. In 1929 a four-month cruise around the world cost a total of . . .
   a. $50
   b. $200
   c. *$900*

Category 2: The Caribbean and the Bahamas[2]

1. In Jamaica, the word *jerk* refers to . . . .
   a. *A special way of barbecuing seasoned meats.*
   b. a type of dance that accompanies reggae music.
   c. a rude driver on local roads.

2. In 1521, Ponce de Leon built a home for his family called Casa Blanca. It is now used as a museum of island life in the early colonial days. On which Caribbean island is this structure found?
   a. *Puerto Rico*
   b. Cuba
   c. Guam

3. Soufriere, an active volcano (3,000 ft high), can be found on which one of the Windward Islands in the Caribbean?
   a. Grenada
   b. *St. Vincent*
   c. Lava Java

4. The string of islands famed as the game-fishing capital of the world, located in the westernmost part of the Bahamian islands, is called . . .
   a. *Bimini Islands.*
   b. Barefoot Islands.
   c. Fisherman Paradise Islands.

5. On Grand Cayman Island is a small bit of landscape that is considered a petrified goo of limestone. Because of its

unusual name, you can send a postcard from a special
postbox which will be marked . . .

   a. Moon

   b. Mars

   c. *Hell*

Category 3: Nautical Terms[3]

1. A boom refers to . . .
   a. a huge noise created when sailors shoot fireworks.
   b. a permanent spar at the foot of the mainsail, fore-sail, or mizzen.
   c. a floating barrier across the entrance to a harbor.
   d. *all of the above*

2. The *mizzen* of a ship is . . .
   a. *the aftermost mast of a vessel.*
   b. slightly bigger than a smizzen.
   c. slang for mezzanine deck level.

3. The *lee* side of a vessel is . . .
   a. the opposite side of the lye side.
   b. the side facing north.
   c. *the side away from the wind.*

4. The *guy* of the ship refers to . . .
   a. a member of the ship's crew that works alongside a mate.
   b. *any wire, chain, or rope used to control the movement of a spar or boom.*
   c. small pole at the bow on which the national flag is hoisted when at anchor.

5. A *scuttle* is . . .
   a. a fight on the main deck.
   b. *the correct name for the window in the side of a ship familiarly known as a porthole.*
   c. a teapot used by the cook.

Category Four: Nautical Distress and Disasters[4]

1. On May 27, 1968, *The US Scorpion,* carrying a crew of 99 officers and men was reported missing. On June 5 she was presumed lost in the depths of the Atlantic with all on board. What was she?
   a. *A nuclear attack submarine*
   b. An aircraft carrier
   c. A runaway spy ship

2. On September 7, 1838, Grace Darling gained fame and notoriety for a heroic act off the Farne Islands. What did she do?
   a. Saved a drowning child from eel-infested waters.
   b. *Rescued 11 survivors from a shipwrecked steamer.*
   c. Saved a dying baby whale.

3. The reason that the *Titanic* carried lifeboats for less than half her complement of passengers and crew was . . .
   a. since she was "unsinkable" the lifeboats were considered unnecessary.
   b. it was an oversight of the shipping company.
   c. *the Board of Trade's regulations at the time did not require any more.*

4. Alexander Selkirk (1676–1721) was a castaway who survived alone for five years on one of the Juan Fernandez islets. His story was the basis for what creative work?
   a. "Gilligan's Island"
   b. <u>*Robinson Crusoe*</u>   ← *correct answer*
   c. *Treasure Island*

5. The famous mystery of the *Mary Celeste* was puzzling because . . .
   a. *the ship was found without any crew or passengers.*
   b. the ship disappeared while at dock.
   c. the ship disappeared while traveling over the Bermuda Triangle.

Category 5: Fish Facts[5]

  1. There are at least _____ kinds of sharks.
      a. 100
      b. *370*
      c. 500

  2. A Regal Tang changes from being completely yellow in its youth to being . . .
      a. brownish with a hint of red.
      b. black and red striped.
      c. *blue with a yellow tail.*

  3. The electric eel . . .
      a. really has no electricity at all.
      b. *makes electricity in special organs, like homemade batteries, which run along the sides of its body.*
      c. gets its electricity from electrolytes in the water.

  4. The wingspan of the mighty manta ray can be more than twenty feet in length, yet he feeds on nothing bigger than . . .
      a. *plankton.*
      b. shrimp.
      c. tripe.

  5. The biggest whale shark on record weighed in at . . .
      a. 2 tons.
      b. 15 tons.
      c. *22 tons.*

Pictures and Favors

Take a group picture before the night is over and send it to the guests as a reminder of this wonderful cruise vacation. If you are interested in giving a small favor bag to your guests as they leave, use light blue bags and include the Polaroid picture taken at arrival. You may want to include some of these items as well: sunglasses, suntan lotion, tropical-flavored Lifesaver candy, small travel log or diary, luggage tags, travel mugs.

Final Note

The vast and mighty waters remind me of God's incredible omniscient power. As a special close to the evening, consider reading the following passage to your passengers, pointing to God as the Lord and Creator of all things.

> There before me lies the mighty ocean, teeming with life of every kind, both great and small. And look! See the ships! And over there, the whale you made to play in the sea. Every one of these depends on you to give them daily food. You supply it, and they gather it. You open wide your hand to feed them and they are satisfied with all your bountiful provision.
>
> PSALM 104:25–28 (TLB)

1. William H. Miller Jr., *The Great Luxury Liners*, (New York: Dover Publications, 1981).

2. James Henderson, *The Caribbean and the Bahamas* (London: Cadogan Books, 1994).

3. Tom Harman, *The Guinness Book of Ships and Shipping Facts* (New York City: Guinness Superlative Ltd., 1983).

4. Harman, *Guinness Book of Ships.*

5. Mary Ling, *Amazing Fish,* (London: Dorling Kindersley Limited, 1993).

Chapter 3

DELICIOUS DESSERT

SWEET SCHEDULE • 1½ HOURS	
20 minutes:	Arrival, coffee, and Candy Bar Icebreaker
50 minutes:	Eat, awards, and Dessertegories
20 minutes:	Talk, laugh, mingle

CAPACITY • 5–25
Consider the purpose of this event. If you want to have a more intimate fellowship, invite 5–8 close friends. If you are planning a large group gathering, this party works just as well for twenty to thirty people.

Did you save room for dessert? This delightful event provides the fantastic opportunity to taste-test a myriad of after-dinner concoctions while enjoying fellowship with friends. Invite your guests to bring their favorite dessert along with the recipe. After the delectable taste test and some delicious coffee, play the unique and exciting new game, Dessertegories.

This is perfect for an after-evening-church fellowship or easy party with neighbors and friends!

Chocolate Invitation

Your invitations will be fun to read and to eat! Purchase a box of flat chocolate bars that have both an inner wrapping and an outer sleeve. Take the outer sleeve off and attach this typewritten invitation in place of the sleeve.

32

PLEASE JOIN US FOR A DELICIOUS TIME
OF DESSERT, COFFEE, FELLOWSHIP, AND FUN!

Date: _____

Time: _____

Place: _____

RSVP: _____

*Bring your best dessert for everyone to taste
and don't forget to bring the recipe!*

Special Note: Are you or your friends counting calories? Make this a Diet Dessert Party. Use a low-fat candy for the invitation and ask your guests to bring their best tasting, lowest fat dessert.

Delicious Decorations

Your decorations will be minimal for this event. Choose one or two colors that you would like to use for your napkins and tablecloth. Consider seasonal colors or ones that fit with your own decor. If you are having a large group, use paper plates; if it is a small gathering, you may want to use your china or dinnerware. For the front door, make a simple "chocolate bar" welcome sign using brown poster board. Cut the poster board in a 10 x 18 rectangle. Glue foil to the ends to look like the wrapping of a chocolate bar. Write "Welcome" on the poster using a white paint pen.

For the centerpiece of your serving table, use a floral arrangement with several candy bars sticking out of it and/or placed around it. Scatter colorful chocolate-coated candies on the table for a confetti-type look. Some stores sell piñatas in the shape of famous candies; these make wonderful decorations as well. The label cards for desserts can be regular name cards with a small candy attached to each one. Write a number on each card. For the Taste Test, ask each guest to place their dessert on the table and write the name of their dessert on the card next to their item.

Name tags can be in the shape of wrapped candies or chocolate kisses. Select background music that suits your taste. I suggest classical or perhaps fifties music.

Arrival Activities

As you greet your guest at the door, show them where to place their dessert on the buffet table. Collect the recipes in a basket to the side. Offer a name tag and a cup of coffee to your guests once their hands are free. Have a table set up as a coffee bar. Since flavored coffees and creams are quite popular, you will have no trouble finding a variety of flavors to provide for your guests. You may need to borrow a few coffee carafes from friends in order to provide a selection. Offer decaf as well as regular coffee for your guests.

You have several options concerning your coffee bar. You may want to provide regular flavored coffee along with a variety of creams and toppings, or you may choose to provide a variety of flavors of coffees instead.

Consider the following:

COFFEE FLAVORS	_COFFEE TOPPINGS_
Regular	Brown sugar
French Blend	Whipped cream
Hazelnut	Cocoa
Mocha	Cinnamon
Créme de menthe	Nutmeg
	Mini-marshmallows
	Maple flavoring
	Vanilla flavoring
	Flavored creams

Cinnamon sticks, peppermint sticks, or chocolate-covered spoons make wonderful stir sticks.

Chocolate-covered spoons can easily be made by using thick, good quality plastic spoons and dipping them into melted chocolate. Set spoons on wax paper to cool to room temperature. Wrap in colored cellophane and tie with a ribbon. These also make great favors or gifts as remembrances of the occasion.

Candy Bar Icebreaker

A fun game to encourage interaction among your guests is to play Candy Bar Create-a-Story. You will need to purchase a variety of candy bars that have distinctive word names used in conversation ($100,000, Butterfinger, Snickers, etc.). Purchase two of each bar. You will also need two black markers and two light-colored poster boards. For each matching set of candy bars, mark one with an *A* and one with a *B*.

Put all of the candy bars into a basket. As guests arrive they are to pick one candy bar, but they are not allowed to eat it yet. Be sure you have enough candy bars to provide one per guest. When you are ready to begin the game, tell everyone with an *A* on their candy to be on one team and everyone with a *B* to be on the other team. The object of the game is to create a short story using the candy bars for words in the story. Each team writes their story using their marker and poster board. When they come to a word that is represented by the candy bar, they will tape the candy bar on the poster board. Give the teams about five minutes to put their story together, then allow each team to read their story to the rest of the group. All participants will enjoy hearing the funny and creative ways people use the candy titles. On this game there are no winners; it is just fun to hear the end products. Allow the participants to keep their candy bars if they so desire.

Time for Dessert

Your Dessert Entry

Here's a wonderful recipe that you can use for the dessert contest:

"The Best" Cheesecake with Strawberry Topping

Crust:

½ cup butter, softened	1 cup enriched flour, sifted
¼ cup sugar	1 tsp lemon peel, grated
1 egg yolk, slightly beaten	¼ tsp vanilla

❖ Combine flour, sugar, and lemon peel. Cut in butter until mixture is crumbly. Add egg yolk and vanilla; blend well. Pat ⅓ of dough on bottom of 9-inch springform pan (with sides removed). Bake for 6–8 minutes in 400° degree oven until golden; cool. Butter sides of pan and attach to bottom. Pat remaining dough evenly on sides to a height of 2 inches.

Cheese Filling:

5 (8 oz) pkgs cream cheese, softened	
1¾ cups sugar	3 Tbsp enriched flour
¾ tsp lemon peel, grated	¼ tsp salt
¼ tsp vanilla	5 eggs
2 egg yolks	¼ cup heavy cream

❖ Beat softened cream cheese until fluffy. Gradually blend next five ingredients into cheese. Add eggs and yolks one at a time, beating well after each. Gently stir in cream. Turn into crust-lined pan. Bake at 500° 5-8 minutes, or until top of crust is golden. Reduce heat to 200° and bake for one hour longer. Remove from oven; cool in pan three hours. Remove sides of pan. Slice and serve with strawberry topping.

Strawberry Topping:

1 pint strawberries	3 Tbsp sugar
1½ Tbsp lemon juice	

❖ Wash and hull strawberries. Put all but six strawberries into electric blender. Add sugar and juice. Process until smooth. Pour into small bowl. Slice remaining 6 strawberries and stir into pureed mixture.
Yields 10–12 slices.

Taste Test

Gather all of your guests to the dessert table for the taste test. Instruct everyone to take a plate and sample as many desserts as they would like. Tell them to consider which dessert they like the best due to taste, appearance, and texture. When most everyone is finished eating, hand out index cards or paper and ask the guests to vote by writing the name of their favorite dessert. You may want to add other prize categories such as Best Looking Dessert, Most Original, Strangest Ingredients, etc. You can present the winners with a collection of chocolate spoons, or small bags of flavored coffee, or a box of chocolates.

Conversation Booster

As your guests enjoy their plateful of desserts, encourage them to discuss this question: "What is the sweetest thing anyone has ever done for you?" This will bring up some interesting stories and conversations.

You may want take this question a step further by mentioning that the Bible says that the greatest love anyone could have for another is to lay down his life for a friend. Jesus did just that for us. Romans 5:6–8 tells us of the nicest thing that anyone has ever done for us: "When we were utterly helpless with no way of escape, Christ came at just the right time and died for us sinners who had no use for him. Even if we were good, we really wouldn't expect anyone to die for us, though, of course, that might be barely possible. But God showed his great love for us by sending Christ to die for us while we were still sinners" (TLB).

Use this opportunity to share the gospel with your guests in a simple way. Allow the Lord to lead you in taking this discussion further.

After-Dessert Fun and Fellowship

Dessertegories

After the taste test and discussion, encourage everyone to refill their coffee and settle in for a short game of Dessertegories. For this game you will need a basket (a hat or bowl will do), a timer, pads of paper, and pencils. Before the party, write the letters of the alphabet on small pieces of paper, one letter per piece excluding x and z. Put the pieces of paper into the basket and hand a pad of paper and pencil to each participant. You can play this game as individuals, pairs, or teams. To choose teams put colored candies in a sack and allow every guest to pick one. They will join the others who have the same colored candy.

The game begins by selecting one Dessert Category listed here:

- Flavors of Ice Cream
- Desserts That Are Served Hot
- Desserts That Are Served Cold
- Types of Coffee
- Desserts That Include Chocolate
- Desserts That Include a Fruit
- Toppings for Ice Cream and Desserts
- Dessert Ingredients

Next, pick one letter from the basket and tell the players the chosen category and the letter. Set the timer for two minutes. Players are to write down as many items fitting the category that start with the given letter. Instruct the participants that they may also think of words that simply contain the given letter, but the word will not be worth as many points. For teams, the team members will work as a group making one list for their team.

Points are awarded for legitimate answers (approved by the other teams). *Twenty points* are awarded for each answer on the list that begins with the given letter and is not matched by any of the other participants. *Ten points* are given for each answer that begins with the given letter but is also found on another participant's list. *One point* will be awarded for each word that includes the given letter somewhere in the word, whether it matches another participant's word or not.

Continue play by selecting another category and choosing a new letter from the basket. Tally up final scores when the game comes to the end. You may want to award winners with a small cookbook or box of chocolates.

Final Note

Collect the recipes brought by each guest and create a small dessert recipe book. Reprint the books and give them to the participants of the party as a remembrance of the special evening. On the night of the party, take a group picture of your guests holding their desserts and use the picture for the cover of your book.

Oh, taste and see that the LORD is good;
Blessed is the man who trusts in Him!

PSALM 34:8

<u>Chapter 4</u>

INCREDIBLE VIDEO SCAVENGER HUNT

SHOOTING SCHEDULE • 2.5 HOURS

When planning the starting time for the party, keep in mind the daylight hours. The videos will turn out better if you have outdoor sunlight, so try to time the party before the sun goes down.

20 Minutes:	Arrival and icebreaker
90 Minutes:	Video Scavenger Hunt
10 Minutes:	Return, snacks, and talk
30 Minutes:	Watch videos (time may vary)

CAMERA CREW CAPACITY: 10–25 PEOPLE

Here's your chance to be a movie star with this fantastically fun video scavenger hunt! Each team will receive a list of imaginative items or actions that must be videotaped as quickly and accurately as possible. When the allotted period of time is over, all the teams will join together for snacks and a look at the video creations from each group. This movie spectacular is a thrill for all ages!

Hollywood Invitations

Invite your friends to be a star with a pair of Hollywood glasses. Purchase inexpensive sunglasses at a discount store, or you can make your own by cutting black poster board in the shape of glasses.

Using ribbon, attach a small card to the glasses. Write the invitation information on the card.

You Are Invited
To Be a Star in an
Incredible Video Scavenger Hunt

Production Stage Location: _____

_____

Taping Time and Date:_____

RSVP to the Director:_____

Invitation alternative: Instead of sunglasses, simply print invitations on bright yellow paper and add star stickers to the paper.

Decorations

Make a big hit with your creative and easy-to-do movie decorations. You can begin at the front door by designing a director's "Take" chart for the door—similar to the chalk chart that directors' assistants click in front of the camera when they say "Take two." You can make your own by cutting black poster board in a rectangle and cutting a small arm that attaches at an angle. Color or paint the arm with white stripes. Write with white paint or chalk, "**INCREDIBLE VIDEO SCAVENGER HUNT, TAKE TWO.**"

See if you can locate a director's chair and a large megaphone for your front porch to enhance the entrance. If you do not have a megaphone available, make one using blue poster board stapled in a cone shape and write **DIRECTOR** down the side.

Movie posters are an easy way to decorate the inside of your home. You can purchase movie posters at some video stores. Theaters may be willing to provide old posters for a minimal cost or free. Be sure to use good taste in selecting your movie posters. You do not want to give the impression that you approve of certain questionable movies.

Using white and black poster boards, create billboard look-alikes to hang on doors and windows. Simply cut the white poster to make a small rectangle framed by the black poster. Use yellow construction paper or paint to create round lights on the black poster. Write with black marker: **"COMING ATTRACTIONS!"**

You may want to use the names of some of your guests for movie titles. For instance: "Carla Conquers the World" or "David's Destiny" or "Smith Family Adventures."

Since your food will be very similar to food at a movie concession stand, a popcorn bucket or bag filled with tissue paper and goodies can make a fun centerpiece. You can save a popcorn bucket from the next time you visit the movies. The centerpiece can also serve as a prize for the winner of the scavenger hunt.

Soundtracks from some of your favorite movies will make the perfect background music during the party. You may also want to play an old black and white classic movie video on the television with the volume turned down.

Arrival Activities

Dress as a movie director to greet your guests. Wear a blazer jacket, beret, and scarf. Hold a small megaphone or clipboard in your hand. Offer beverages and encourage your guests to mingle. After most of the guests have arrived gather them together to play an icebreaker game called "Costar Mixer."

Costar Mixer

Before the party you will need to make movie tickets using colored construction paper. On each movie ticket write two costars' names from either current movies or old classics. Both names should be on one ticket and the letters in the names should be scrambled. Cut the tickets in half, cutting each one slightly different from the others in jigsaw fashion. When each guest arrives, he or she will receive one half of the ticket. The players must find their match by matching together the jagged edges.

Once the players have found their match, then they must unscramble the letters together with their partner. Any couple who is able to identify the costars on their ticket will win a small prize, such as candy, inexpensive sunglasses, or an autograph pen.

The Incredible Video Scavenger Hunt

Divide into Teams

Before the party you will need to ask several people (safe drivers) to act as designated drivers for the big scavenger hunt. Calculate how many drivers you will need considering the amount of guests participating. Each team should have at least four people. To divide into groups put all of the participant's names (except for drivers) into a popcorn bucket or bag. Each driver will pull the amount of names that he has room for in his car. Each car can represent a team or you can couple cars together to form a team. Married people should be grouped with their spouses. If you have invited entire families to the party, then each family will be a team. What a great time for family bonding!

Distribute Video Cameras

You will need to plan ahead to have a blank videotape and a video camera for each group. Ask several friends to bring their cameras along, batteries charged and ready to go. Call your friends a few hours before the party just to remind them to bring their camera, or collect them the day before. Be sure that everyone has labeled their camera.

Because there is such a variety of videotape sizes available for different cameras, you will need to consider making provisions for the different tape sizes. Some tapes come with playback video cartridges, while other video recorders hook up directly to the television. Check to make sure that you will be able to watch each production one way or another. You don't want a group to be disappointed because they cannot view their movie.

Alternative Options: This party works well with still-shot pictures too! If video cameras are hard to come by, use Polaroid cameras and make this a photo scavenger hunt.

Introduce the Game
Basically there are four rules.

1. Every person in your group must appear in each video scene. They can take turns operating the camera.

2. Safety and kindness outweigh speed. Although there are small rewards for completing the list first, it is not worth the cost of dangerous driving or rudeness to strangers.

3. You must attempt to complete each action on the list and return by the designated time. (As the host, you will need to determine a reasonable and safe amount of time to accomplish the given tasks. Consider safety first! You do not want to make the participants dash wildly around town to accomplish a long list in a short amount of time. Make a practice run-through in your town to help you determine the time frame.) The first team to return with all of the items complete will receive bonus points. If no team completes all of the list, then points will be awarded to the team that completes the most.

4. Have fun!

Pray together as a group before you start. Pray for safety and Christlike examples within the competition. Use the scavenger hunt list provided in this chapter or make up your own list using locations and items specifically found in your city. You will need to type the list and give each team a copy. To build anticipation, put the list in a secret envelope only to be opened when you give the signal. Some video stores give away old empty plastic video cases. Use the cases instead of envelopes as a unique way to hand out the scavenger list.

Note: Depending on your group and the list of items that you choose, you may need to consider setting an expense limit.

Tell your guests that they may spend no more than $\$$_____ per group. A budget adds to the creativity and fun of the event. If you do not want them to spend any money, then you will need to provide art supplies and picnic items for them.

Scavenger Hunt List

1. *Movie Title.* Every great movie has an exciting title and introduction. As a team, decide on the title of your production. Creatively present the title on your video. Feel free to use posters, signs, or banners. Be creative with your background setting and make sure that everyone (except camera person) is included in the shot. Extra points for the most original presentation.

2. *Grocery Store.* Videotape each team member holding a different product starting with the letter *Y* in a local grocery store. Extra points for videotaping the cashier holding a "Y" product as well.

3. *Athletic Event.* Videotape your group watching an athletic event of any kind (create your own if you cannot find one). Extra points given if one of your members is taped cheering for a team at the event.

4. *Restaurant.* Videotape your group eating at a restaurant (any type). Each member must be filmed taking a bite of food. You must show the name of the restaurant in your video. Extra points awarded for taping one of your members acting as a waitress serving food.

★★ Alternative: Provide simple picnic fixings for each group and instruct them to videotape their group eating their picnic. Extra points for the most unique location for the picnic.

5. *Skit.* Perform a short skit portraying a great classic or Bible story. Extra points if you use costumes.

6. *Hats.* Using newspaper and tape provided, each member must create a hat and model it for the video. Extra points awarded for the group whose member creates the tallest hat.

7. *Statues.* Visit a statue, fountain, or monument and videotape your group standing by it. Extra points awarded for creating your own human monument at the scene of the one you are visiting.

8. *Videos.* Visit a video store. Each player must find a video that starts with the same letter as the first letter of his/her name. Extra points awarded if the videos are all musicals.

Point Value

The point system works as follows. Each group will receive ten points for a completed item on the list. Five points for each bonus item. The team that finishes first (or completes the most in the allotted time) receives an extra five points. Judging and tallying of scores will take place when you watch the video.

Food and Fellowship

As everyone returns to your home, collect and label their videos. You will need to make a special effort to return to your house first or tell each team where they can find the key to your house. Provide snacks that are found at the concession stand of a movie theater, such as bags of popcorn, a variety of soft drinks, and candies.

Conversation Booster

Encourage conversation by asking people to share the funniest thing that happened to their group during the hunt. You will find that everyone will enjoy talking about their adventures and the funny things that happened to them.

It's Showtime

After every team has arrived and you have given adequate time for getting snacks and sharing, gather everyone to the television for the viewing and judging of the videos. Be sure to have pen and paper to tally the score for each group as you watch the productions.

Awards Ceremony

After viewing the videos provide an awards ceremony similar to the Academy Awards. Give awards for not only the highest accumulated points, but also Best Actor and Actress, Comedy Award, Best Photography, and so on. You may want to give away the popcorn bucket centerpieces or present ribbons or small plastic trophies found at party stores. For the grand prize give gift certificates or coupons to a local video store or theater.

Closing Credits

You may choose to share this closing thought with all of your guests. It is amusing and sometimes scary to see ourselves on video. Can you imagine if all of our deeds were videotaped on camera? That would tend to change our attitudes, language, and actions, wouldn't it?

Although we are not being videotaped at all times (thank goodness!), there is someone always watching over us. God is the God who sees all. He knows what we have been through and what we have done, and loves us anyway. How comforting to realize that even when no one else seems to understand, God knows, sees, and understands.

Final Note

This is a wonderful party to build group and/or family togetherness. Be sensitive to more reserved individuals and adjust any items on the scavenger hunt list that your guests may find embarrassing or silly. The intent of this party is not to embarrass your guests but to build teamwork and relationships. You know your guests best so judge accordingly. Also, encourage good sportsmanship and clean competition, and most importantly, have fun!

> O LORD, You have searched me and known me.
> You know my sitting down and my rising up;
> You understand my thought afar off.
>
> PSALM 139:1–2

Chapter 5

COOK BY THE BOOK

SCRUMPTIOUS SCHEDULE • ALMOST 2 HOURS

20 Minutes:	Arrival, add ingredients, mingle
20 Minutes:	Mystery Ingredients Game while stew is cooking
60 Minutes:	Enjoy meal, coffee and fellowship

HOW MANY COOKS IN THE KITCHEN? • 8–15

Cook up a great party by inviting your guests to bring the ingredients to a special Friendship Stew. This unique party allows the guests to do the cooking and the end result is a delicious meal accompanied by intriguing conversation! Here's an easy way to have dinner with friends without a tremendous amount of preparation.

Invitations from the Chief Chef

Flat plastic or wooden cooking spoons or scrapers are inexpensive and make great invitations. Men enjoy trying their hand in the kitchen too, so do not be hesitant about inviting them. Write the party information on a recipe card and attach the card to the kitchen utensil using ribbon. The recipe card alone could be used for your invitation just as well. Here's what to say:

Recipe for COOKING PARTY

From the Kitchen of: _____*your name*_____

Ingredients:

    1 houseful of wonderful friends
       Large bowls of Friendship Stew
    1 pound of great conversation

Instructions:

❖ Gather friends together at ___*time*___ on ___*day, date*___.
❖ Each guest brings one ingredient to help create a savory stew.
❖ Once food has been prepared, all guests will join together to enjoy the delectable delight.
❖ Sprinkle entire event with joyful fellowship.
❖ Serve at: _____*your address*_____
❖ When you RSVP you will find out the important ingredient that you are to bring, ___*phone number*___.

As your guests begin to call with their RSVP assign them an ingredient from the Friendship Stew recipe. Keep a careful list of who is bringing which ingredient. If you have a smaller group, some people may need to bring more than one item for the stew (see page 52 for stew ingredients).

Tasteful Decorations

You can find most of your decorations in your own kitchen. Use pitchers, carafes, vases, or even painted coffee cans to hold bouquets of flowers along with a few kitchen utensils. You can use fresh flowers or artificial. Trim with ribbons or a bow that coordinates with the tablecloths. Cookbooks can be excellent decorative items as well. Stand them up in various places around the house—on coffee and end tables and next to the centerpieces on the dining tables.

This event works best as a sit-down dinner, so try to create dining space by adding card tables covered with tablecloths, as well as your own dining and kitchen tables. Use your own tablecloths or purchase several inexpensive checkered cloths that blend with your color scheme. If possible use your own dinnerware. If you have more people than you have plates and you want to make cleanup quicker, use plastic plates that coordinate with your colors. Don't forget bowls and spoons for the stew.

Name cards at the tables will help everyone find their place and encourage new friendships. Make simple place cards by using illustrated recipe cards. Write the names of your guests on the cards and stand the cards up by attaching a small piece of poster board to the back of the recipe card and folding the board back. You may also choose to use small plastic frames to hold the cards. For background music, play Italian or French music.

Chefs' hats, called toques, make another great decoration. You can find chefs' hats at restaurant or kitchen supply stores. Set the hats around the house and the kitchen for decoration. Create a sign for your door that says, "*WELCOME TO COOKING WITH (YOUR NAME)!*" Use sturdy, colored poster board and attach a chef's hat with a couple of wooden spoons to the sign. If budget allows, give each guest a chef's hat or apron as they arrive.

Arrival Activities

Add Ingredients

Designate one cohost or friend to greet as another cohost supervises stew preparations in the kitchen. The greeter should welcome with a smile, offer to take coats, and point the way to the kitchen. Once in the kitchen, your guests will add their ingredient to the stew. Offer soft drinks or punch and allow everyone to mingle until most of the guests (and ingredients) have arrived. Play the Mystery Ingredient Game as the stew is cooking.

Mystery Ingredient Game

For this delicious game you will need to prepare three different hors d'oeuvres. (For recipes, see "appetizers" in index of this book.) Place an index card by each hors d'oeuvre listing the ingredients, yet purposely leave off one ingredient from each card. The object of the game is for the participants to taste each of the three hors d'oeuvres and try to figure out which ingredient has been omitted from each card. Select several recipes using the index in the back of the book.

Give each player a piece of paper with the numbers one, two, and three down the left side of the page. Ask each player to write their guesses for the missing ingredients. Give small prizes to those who guess correctly. Prizes can be pot holders, wooden spoons, measuring cups or spoons or refrigerator magnets.

Chef's Menu

Orange Almond Salad
Friendship Stew
Make-Ahead Refrigerator Rolls
Chocolate Company Cake

Dressing:

½ cup oil	3 Tbsp red wine vinegar
1 Tbsp lemon juice	2 Tbsp sugar,
½ tsp salt	½ tsp dry mustard

❖ Shake together and refrigerate.
❖ You can make this dressing several days before the party.

Salad:
    1 (11 oz) can mandarin oranges, drained
    1 bunch Romaine, Boston, or leaf lettuce
    ½ red onion, thinly sliced   ¼ cup slivered almonds, toasted

❖ Toss together lettuce and onion. Sprinkle almonds and oranges on the top. Add dressing and lightly toss entire salad minutes before serving.
❖ Yields 8-10 servings.

Try these delicious rolls that can be prepared a few days before the party or use your own favorite dinner rolls or bread.

Friendship Stew

2 lbs ground beef, browned and drained
4 (16 oz) cans Italian-style crushed tomatoes
2 medium onions, peeled and coarsely chopped
1 (16 oz) can yellow corn   1 (16 oz) can green beans
1 (8¼ oz) can sliced carrots   2 tsp salt
1 tsp black pepper   1 tsp crushed oregano
1 (6 oz) pkg frozen green peas

❖ Combine all ingredients except for peas and bring to a boil; reduce heat. Simmer stew slowly for 15-20 minutes. Add peas and cook 5 minutes longer. You may add 4 potatoes (peeled, chopped, and cooked) or cooked noodles to this recipe as well.
❖ Serve salad and bread along with the stew.
❖ Yields 8-10 servings.

Make-Ahead Refrigerator Rolls

2 cups warm water   2 yeast cakes
1 cup sugar   2 eggs
6 cups flour   1 cup oil
1 Tbsp salt

❖ Mix yeast in warm water until dissolved. Add sugar, eggs, oil, and salt. Add flour, a little at a time. Turn dough onto floured board and knead. Put into large bowl and cover. Refrigerate. Dough will keep for about 2 weeks. Before cooking, take the amount of dough that you need out of refrigerator, form into 1 inch balls and allow to rise for 2½–3 hours or until double in size. Bake at 425° for 15 minutes.

Chocolate Company Cake

2 (21 oz) pkg brownie mix   2 eggs, beaten
1 cup cooking oil   1 cup water
1½ cups walnuts

❖ Combine all ingredients, mixing well. Pour into 9 x 13-inch greased baking pan. Bake at 350° for 40 minutes.

Frosting:
1 stick margarine   ¼ cup milk
4 tsp cocoa   1 lb powdered sugar
1 tsp vanilla   1 cup walnuts

❖ Melt margarine in a large saucepan. Add milk and cocoa and stir over low heat until smooth. Remove from heat and gradually add powdered sugar, stirring with wire whisk until blended. Stir in vanilla and nuts. Mix well and pour over warm cake.

❖ Yields 15–18 servings.

Conversation Booster

When the food is ready, ask everyone to sit down and offer a prayer of thanks for the food. You may want to encourage interaction between the guests by writing a question on the back of each place card. Wonderful conversations and new friendships are sometimes born out of simple questions. Here are several suggestions:

- Where is your favorite vacation spot?
- What is your fondest childhood memory?
- Who is the most important person in your life and why?
- What is the title of the most recent book you have read?
- Where would you like to live if you didn't live in this city?
- Name someone you do not know but would like to meet.
- What kind of music do you like to listen to?
- What is the last movie you have seen in a theater?
- What is your idea of a great date night?

After-Dinner Fellowship

Dessert

After dinner, collect the plates and serve coffee and dessert. You may want to move everyone away from the table and into the living room for coffee and dessert, since this is a time to relax and visit. If you would like an after-dinner activity, try the "Who

Am I?" game. Remember this is only optional and not necessary. If you see that conversations are going well at the tables, then serve coffee and dessert and encourage the fellowship.

"Who Am I?" Game

Hand out slips of paper and pens to every guest and ask them to write down a little-known or unique fact about themselves. This can be something in the present or that happened in their past. It can apply to an accomplishment or a talent or even a special place they have visited. After a few minutes, collect the slips and put them in a mixing bowl. One by one pick a slip from the bowl and read it out loud. Allow two minutes for people to guess who it describes. At the end of two minutes, if the person has not been guessed then he must reveal who he is. This game presents a great opportunity to get to know a little more about your guests. You may be surprised at what you find out!

Final Note

The Friendship Stew presents a marvelous object lesson and reminder that as believers God can use each of us for His kingdom. Just as it was important to have every guest contribute a different ingredient to the stew, so each Christian contributes unique talents, gifts and abilities to the body of Christ.

Isn't it amazing what you can learn from a pot of stew?!

Now God gives us many kinds of special abilities, but it is the same Holy Spirit who is the source of them all. There are different kinds of service to God, but it is the same Lord we are serving. There are many ways in which God works in our lives, but it is the same God who does the work in and through all of us who are his. The Holy Spirit displays God's power through each of us as a means of helping the entire church.

1 CORINTHIANS 12:4–7, TLB

Chapter 6

BACK TO SCHOOL DAYS

SCHOOL SCHEDULE • 2 HOURS

20 Minutes:	*Arrival, Graduate Guessing Game*
40 Minutes:	*School Food!*
60 Minutes:	*Dessert and games*

HIGH SCHOOL ENROLLMENT: 10-40 STUDENTS

It's a blast from the past with a high school memories party! Play nostalgic games and enjoy a dinner in the high school cafeteria. Your guests are invited to dress as they once did in high school and show off their old yearbooks and pictures. Ice cream sundaes, memorable activities, and reflection on priorities will cap off the evening!

Invitations by Diploma

Using paper with a border that resembles a certificate or diploma (found at office supply stores), type the following information:

  <u>your last name</u> mont High School Diploma

Example:

> ### LADDMONT HIGH SCHOOL DIPLOMA
> *This hereby certifies that the bearer of this diploma*
> *is invited to return to the memories of high school*
> *at a party on the _____ day of _____*
> *at the time of _____.*

The bearer of this diploma must meet the requirements of
searching for high school yearbooks, pictures,
and clothes from yesteryear.
Graduate must dress as he did in high school
and be accompanied by paraphernalia of nostalgic memories.

Laddmont High School Address:

_____

RSVP to the Principal: _____

Dinner will be served in the High School Cafeteria.

Decorations

Place high school memorabilia in the center of each table. Items such as footballs, pom-poms, notebooks, band instruments, old textbooks (found at book resale shops), rulers, and megaphones will all add to the look. Sprinkle confetti on the table around the decorations to add color. Your tablecloths can be plain and simple. Butcher paper or plastic will be fine since we want to create the feel of a high school cafeteria. Use metal folding chairs at the table to add to that "cafeteria look."

For place cards, set miniature chalkboards (found at craft stores) at each setting and use white paint to write your guests' names. If small chalkboards are not in your budget, make your own using black poster board and brown construction paper as a frame to the board. Place a piece of chalk and a bright red apple at each place setting.

Set old yearbooks and other memorabilia (listed above) around the house on coffee tables and end tables. On the walls place butcher paper banners cheering on the high school's team. Attach homemade or actual school pennants to the walls. If you can find letter jackets and sweaters either in your own closet or at resale shops, drape them on several chairs.

Put classroom signs on the doors of different rooms in your home. For the kitchen door put a sign that reads, "SCHOOL

LUNCHROOM." Place signs on the rest room door that read, "Boys Restroom," "Girls Restroom." Write tasteful graffiti on paper tacked to the walls inside the rest rooms—phrases such as "Sally Loves Johnny," or "I hate homework!" Leave pens and room on the paper for your guests to add to the graffiti.

For your entrance use a large foam poster board placed above the door. This is supposed to look like an official sign that displays the name of your school (example: LADDMONT HIGH). Attach a chalkboard or butcher paper banner to the front door that says, "WELCOME BACK TO SCHOOL!"

Arrival Activities

Photograph Your Guests

Greet your guests at the door by welcoming them back to school. Give each guest a name tag in the shape of a small school pennant as they arrive. Take pictures of your guests in front of a well-decorated area. Try to locate some old lockers at a secondhand shop. These would make a great decoration as well as a good spot for photos.

Graduate Guessing Game

For the Guessing Game you will need to do some preparation before the party. When your friends call to RSVP, ask them to tell you a little-known fact about themselves in high school. Perhaps it is an award they won or a position they held or something funny or significant that they did. If you have invited couples, you will need to get information about the spouse as well. Type the information on one page without revealing the names. Make enough copies for each of your guests.

When guests arrive at the party, give them the list of information and a yellow school pencil. The object of the game is to chat with people at the party and try to discover who fits with what item on the list. When most people have completed or attempted to complete the page, gather all of the guests together to give the correct answers. Allow time for any explanations that someone may want to give concerning the information on the sheet. Award a small prize to the people who completed their list. Awards can be as simple as a colorful note pad, plastic football, pen and pencil set, or an apple.

Cafeteria Menu

Plate Lunch	*Sack Lunch*	*Dessert*
Tossed Salad	*Apple*	*Ice Cream Sundaes*
Spaghetti	*Sub sandwich*	
Garlic Bread	*Bag of Chips*	

Ring a bell or buzzer to signal mealtime. Tell your guests that they will need to line up to get their food in the "lunch room." Offer two options to your guests. They may choose from either a plate lunch special or a sack lunch. Serve the plate lunch on trays. You may be able to find divided trays at a party store or restaurant supply. If you or one of your friends feel so inclined, dress up as a funny lunchroom lady to serve the food to your guests. Wear a hair net, thick-rimmed glasses, rubber gloves, and a solid-colored pastel outfit.

For the plate lunch, provide spaghetti, garlic bread, and tossed salad. (The plate lunch that stands out most in my memory is cutlet with mashed potatoes and gravy. Since I'm not quite sure what that "cutlet" was, I won't recommend it as an option for this party.) The sack lunch will contain a sub sandwich, bag of chips, and an apple. Try to find small cartons of milk or other juice drinks in cartons. Lemonade will work just as well.

Conversation Booster
Instruct your class that during meal time they are allowed to talk with their neighbors. As a conversation booster ask your guests to discuss what was the most important thing to them in high school (grades, dating, honors, cheerleading, etc.). Then ask them to compare it to what is important now in their life.

After-Dinner Fun and Fellowship

When finished eating, students should be instructed to take their trays to the kitchen or throw away their sack lunches. During the game time that follows, make a quick change of signs on the kitchen so that the kitchen sign now reads, "Malt Shop."

Several activities are provided here. Choose the games that best fit your group's personality.

Talent Show

When your guests RSVP, ask them if they have any talents that they would like to share with the group. Perhaps they played the saxophone or twirled a baton in their high school years. Encourage them to bring what they need to present their talent in the show. You can even type a simple Talent Show program before the party listing all of the acts. You will be amazed at the hidden talents that lie dormant within your friends!

This is also a good time for anyone to show some of the memorabilia that they brought to the party. Everyone will get a kick out of looking at old pictures and yearbooks.

Name that Tune!

Guests of all ages love this nostalgic game! Before the party, make a tape recording of several old familiar songs. They may be popular songs from past decades or theme songs from famous television programs. Music stores and bargain book-stores are a good resource for old tunes. Divide into two teams or play men against women. Set two chairs in the front of the room, one designated for each team. Play a small segment of a song and when a team member knows the title to the tune, he will run and sit in his team chair to give the answer. (It is a good rule to say that no one can answer two times in a row.)

Each team receives one point for a correct answer. If a team member answers incorrectly, then the other team has an opportunity to answer. Points are tallied at the end of play and the winning team receives a small prize, such as bubble gum or a candy bar. You may want to prepare between fifteen and twenty songs for the game and be sure to play them loud enough for all participants to hear.

Go to the Head of the Class

Use the game of Quotable Quotes found in chapter 10 of this book. Call the game "Go to the Head of the Class" for this party. Divide the group into two teams according to the year of graduation. If a guest's graduation year is an odd number he is on Team One, and if the graduation year is even then he is on Team Two. Ask a question to one team—if they get it right they receive five points; if they do not get it right the question goes to the other team. The team with the most points is the winner.

Dictionary

This is an old game that has been passed on from generation to generation. It can be played with teams or as individuals. You will need a dictionary, pencils, and paper for this game. Players take turns looking up unfamiliar words in the dictionary. They will read the true definition and make up a false one. Everyone then guesses by secret ballot which definition they think is the true one. A person wins one point when she guesses the true definition. One point is awarded to the reader if someone guesses his false definition as true. Points are tallied at the end of play and prizes awarded for the highest number of points. Prizes can be a pocket dictionary, colorful pencils, pad and pen, etc.

Dessert!

At some point between games, announce that the Malt Shop is open and is offering free ice cream sundaes. Provide bowls, spoons, and a variety of ice creams and toppings. Allow guests to create their own sundaes. Here's a fantastic fudge sauce to help make the ice cream sundaes a big success:

Dodson's Chocolate Fudge Topping

From the kitchen of Sherry Dodson

½ cup cocoa	1 cup sugar
1 cup light corn syrup	½ cup evaporated milk
¼ tsp salt	3 Tbsp margarine
1 tsp vanilla	

❖ Combine all ingredients except vanilla in a saucepan. Cook over medium heat, stirring constantly until mixture comes to a full boil. Boil 3 minutes. Remove from heat; add vanilla. Serve hot.

❖ Yields 2½ cups.

School's Out

As the party comes to a close, present your guests with a "Back to School" party favor bag. Use colorful red and blue bags lined with yellow tissue paper. Fill the bags with an apple, several pencils, a note pad, and a plastic football. Add a card or note with Proverbs 1:7 on it, "The fear of the LORD is the beginning of knowledge." Don't forget to add the place card chalkboards and any Polaroid pictures taken at the party.

Final Note

After the party, send your guests a homemade yearbook made up of pictures taken at the event. Write Philippians 3:13 on the front cover. Isn't it exciting to know that God is a God of moving forward and not dwelling in the past?

> Forgetting what lies behind and reaching forward to what lies ahead, I press on toward the goal for the prize of the upward call of God in Christ Jesus.
>
> PHILIPPIANS 3:13–14, NASB

<u>*Chapter 7*</u>

THE
BEST WESTERN

COWBOY COUNTDOWN • 2 HOURS	
20 minutes:	Arrival, pictures, horseshoes, bandana toss
50 minutes:	Barbecue Buffet
50 minutes:	Howdy Bingo

CAPACITY: 10-40 COWBOYS & COWGIRLS

Git yer cowboy boots and hat for a cotton-pickin' good time at the Best Western Party this side of the Pecos! Enjoy a game of horseshoes, a Bandito Bandana Toss, a Branding Iron Contest and a round of Cowboy Bingo. The delicious Bar-B-Que chicken, baked beans, spoon bread, and home-made apple pie are sure to make this a western night to remember!

"Wanted" Poster Invitations

Old West "Wanted Posters" will make a perfect invitation to this western shindig. Use 8 x 10 parchment paper found at office supply stores. Brown packaging paper can also be used by cutting 8 x 10 rectangles. I prefer parchment paper because it will run through the printer or copier. Type or print the information below in Old West style font:

W A N T E D
GUEST'S NAME

**MIRROR
SQUARE**

To show up at that there Best Western Party
this side of the Pecos!

Mark yer calendar fer: _____date_____
Rootin, Tootin Time: _____time_____
Ranch Location: _____address_____
Let us know if yer comin: _____phone number_____

WEAR YER WEST'RN DUDS!

Cut a small (2 x 3) rectangle out of aluminum foil and glue it to the center of the poster to act as a mirror. You may be able to find some inexpensive plastic mirrors to attach instead or perhaps a funny drawing or picture. Burn the edges of the wanted poster with matches to give it an Old West look. Send the invitations flat in large brown envelopes. You can send folded invitations in regular envelopes, but watch the mirror to keep it from bending.

Ranch-Style Decorations

Place bales of hay at your entrance accompanied by cowboy boots, a hat, and a guitar. Bales of hay can be purchased at a feed store. If you do not own a guitar, see if you can borrow one or use a toy guitar that looks real. Purchase a large number of bandanas or bandana material (cut in triangles) and tie them everywhere—door knobs, lamps, vases, candlesticks, etc. You will also need several bolts of rope or twine. The rope can be placed in the center of the table surrounding a flower arrangement. A cowboy boot with bandana and artificial bluebonnet flowers inside makes a perfect centerpiece. Scatter dried pinto and red beans on the table as extra decorations.

Use thin twine at your table to tie the napkins with your silver or plastic dinnerware. Use either bandanas or red paper napkins. If budget allows, Mason jars are perfect for drinks, otherwise red plastic cups will do the trick. Tablecloths can be red checked or denim material or they can be solid red or blue.

Hang silver stars from the ceilings and place them on the walls. Play your favorite country-western music. (There are some fantastic Christian country-western tapes available at Christian bookstores.) If you have any old metal tubs (available at feed stores), fill them with ice and bottles of root beer for your guests to enjoy as they arrive.

Arrival Activities

As your guests arrive at the door, greet them with a big "Howdy" and a handshake. Give each guest a sheriff's badge name tag. You can purchase toy sheriff badges from party stores. Under the word *Sheriff* write your guest's name using marker or paint pen, or write on a strip of white tape attached to the pin. Offer bottled root beer or large glasses of lemonade for your guests as they arrive. Set up a station called the "Watering Hole" with drinks available.

Take Pictures

Encourage your guests to have their pictures taken in a specially designated spot. Set up a special area with bales of hay. Before the party, ask one of your friends (preferably a camera buff) to take pictures or hire the work done professionally. Other ideas for backdrop or scenery include a wagon wheel, picket fence, and a wooden board that is cut and painted to resemble a cow. Provide a pair of cowboy hats and bandanas at the camera site for those people who did not wear their own.

Home on the Range Horseshoes

Set up a game of horseshoes in a grassy area. You can find horseshoe sets at most toy stores or look for more authentic ones at specialty shops. Depending on how many guests you have invited you may want to have more than one game going.

Bandito Bandana Toss

Another game that you can play outdoors or indoors (if the weather is bad) is a bandana toss. You will need several bandanas, rubber bands, and pennies. Put five pennies in the center of a bandana, gather the ends and secure with a rubber band, leaving a tail to the bandana game piece. Make as many as you like. Set a round lasso loop made of twine or rope in a large open space several yards from the starting position. Players hold the bandana by the tail, and toss it attempting to land the coin filled bandana in the circle.

Livestock Lasso

Allow your guests to try their hand with a lasso. Set up a chair (decorated with cardboard to look like a cow would be cute) and provide medium-sized rope. Secure a loop in the rope and mark off a line several feet from the cow chair. Let your guests take turns attempting to lasso the cow. Place this activity away from the main mingling area, as you do not want an unsuspecting guest to be lassoed by mistake.

Barbecue Buffet Menu

New Potato Salad
Barbecued Chicken
Baked Beans
Spoon Bread
Homestyle Apple Pie and Ice Cream

Chow time! Ring a large dinner bell to gather your guests for prayer and vittles.

New Potato Salad

8-10	large new potatoes	3	green onions, chopped
⅓	cup chopped fresh parsley	¼	cup olive oil
¼	cup lemon juice	1	tsp salt
	dash of garlic powder		dash of pepper

❖ Scrub potatoes with vegetable brush and cook in boiling water (with skins on) for 20–25 minutes or until tender. Drain and cool. Cut potatoes into wedges and combine with onions and parsley. Mix remaining ingredients; pour over potato mixture, tossing gently. Chill at least 3 hours.

❖ Yields 8-10 servings.

Barbecued Chicken

3 cups cider vinegar	4 Tbsp margarine
1½ Tbsp black pepper	1 Tbsp minced garlic
9 Tbsp Worcestershire sauce	3 Tbsp shortening
½ Tbsp chili powder	2 dashes of Tabasco
2 tsp salt	
6 chicken halves, lightly salted and peppered	

❖ Combine all ingredients except chicken in a saucepan and bring to a boil. Turn down and simmer for 10 minutes or more. Sauce can be refrigerated in a jar for several weeks. Marinate chicken overnight in sauce. Place chicken in a 350° oven or on an enclosed barbecue grill. Baste the chicken with sauce every 15 minutes and turn every 30 minutes. Do not place chicken directly over coals. Cook 1–1½ hours. Cooking time may vary according to your grill.

Baked Beans

3 slices of bacon, cut in half	2 (16 oz) cans pork and beans
1 cup packed brown sugar	1 cup catsup
1 medium onion, chopped	¼ cup Worcestershire Sauce
2 Tbsp mustard	

❖ Partially cook bacon. Combine the rest of the ingredients and put in casserole dish. Lay bacon on top. Bake at 325° uncovered for 2 hours or until desired consistency.

❖ Yields 10–12 servings.

Spoon Bread

1 stick margarine	1 (8 oz) package cornbread
1 egg	8 oz sour cream
1 (16 oz) can kernel corn, drained	

❖ Melt margarine in a large saucepan. Add the rest of the ingredients, mixing well. Put in 8 x 8 greased baking dish. Bake at 350° for 30–40 minutes until set and lightly browned on top.

❖ Yields 8-10 servings.

Homestyle Apple Pie

6–8 cups Granny Smith apples, peeled and thinly sliced
1   cup sugar   2   Tbsp flour
1   tsp cinnamon   ⅛   tsp nutmeg
¼   tsp salt   2   Tbsp butter or margarine
2   pie crusts

❖ Combine sugar, flour, cinnamon, nutmeg, and salt and mix
  lightly through apples. Place in pastry-lined 9 inch pie pan.
  Dot with butter. Place second crust on top and flute edges.
  Cut vents. Bake at 400° for 50 minutes or until crust is
  brown and apples are tender. Top with ice cream or
  whipped cream.

This is the perfect occasion for some good old-fashioned
homemade ice cream!

Conversation Booster
Just as cowboys had a challenging job on the open range, life
in the city has its challenges as well. Cowboys sat around the
campfire singing and telling stories to relax from a hard day of
work. Ask your guests to discuss this question over dinner:
"What do you find challenging in your life and what do you
do to relax after a hard day?"

Later in the evening you can extend the discussion by
saying that in a world full of cares, it is important to know that
God cares for us. He wants us to cast all of our cares on Him.
Psalm 55:22 says, "Cast your burden on the LORD, and He
shall sustain you." How comforting it is to realize that in a busy
and burdened society our hearts can find rest in Jesus. He truly
cares for us!

After-Dinner Fun and Fellowship

Howdy Bingo
Create your own bingo cards using pictures and words that
apply to cowboys and ranch life. You will need twenty-five
pictures or words to go in the squares. Use simple black and

white drawings or graphics of pictures such as a star, rope, tin cup, horseshoe, cow, sunset, campfire, boots, cowboy hat. Use words such as *giddyap, ride'em cowboy, whoa,* and *shoot-out,* in some of the squares. Arrange the pictures differently on six different cards. Each card will have five spaces down and five across, with the word *howdy* in the center. Copy the cards as many times as you need according to the number of guests at your party.

Mount the playing cards on cardboard and laminate them or put them in plastic sleeves. Use buttons for the markers on the cards. You can purchase bags of odd buttons at a craft store or fabric shop. Put one set of pictures in a cowboy hat or boot. Draw out one picture at a time and allow everyone to place a button on the corresponding picture on their gameboard. Winners must have five across, although you can play variations such as four corners or four edges. You will have several winners at the same time since several people will have duplicate game boards. This will keep the game moving. The more winners the better. Play bingo several times, mixing the cards between each game to provide the opportunity for a variety of winners.

Branding Iron Bonanza
(Idea by Mrs. Dana Crawford)
Give each player a two-foot, easily bendable wire—floral wire would be a good choice. Tell your guests that they are going to create their own branding iron including their initials. The contestants will have three minutes to make their branding iron. When time is up, show the results so that everyone can see the final products. You may want to award prizes for most creative, best use of wire, originality, first to finish, etc.

Wild West Show
On slips of paper, write old Western roles that can be acted out. For instance: herding cattle, singing by the campfire, driving a stagecoach, plowing fields, milking a cow. Place all of the slips of paper in a cowboy hat. Pass around the hat for each player to draw one slip. Each player takes a turn role-playing the

action on his or her paper. Everyone must guess what the exact wording was on the paper. Five points will be awarded to the first person to guess the action correctly. Five points will also be awarded to the actor or actress who is able to have the action guessed within forty-five seconds. Award prizes for the person with the highest points, the most imaginative performance, and the funniest actor or actress. Create as many awards as you like.

Cowboy Chalk Talk
You will need a large chalkboard and several pieces of white chalk. Use the same idea as the Wild West Show, but instead of acting out what is on the slip of paper, each guest will take a turn drawing the given action on the chalkboard.

Prize Ideas for Games
Put prizes in brown paper lunch sacks, folded at the top. Punch two holes and thread twine through the holes and tie. Depending on your budget, prizes could be chocolate candies, plastic mugs, small cowboy key chains, or homemade cookies in the shape of stars or boots.

Final Note

Western parties offer a wonderful, casual atmosphere for fellowship. There are many Western activities other than games. Most towns have a square dance caller who will bring his own music for a night of do-si-dos. Perhaps you have a humorous speaker at your church that you would like to invite to give a light message. A local guitar player can entertain guests as well. If you are in an outdoor area that allows for a campfire, spend time singing and telling stories around the campfire. If children will be involved in this event you may want to check out the possibility of pony rides or a hay ride.

Y'all have a good time now, ya hear?!

Rejoice in the Lord always. Again I will say, rejoice!
PHILIPPIANS 4:4

Chapter 8

MAUI WOWEE

LUAU SCHEDULE• 1.5 HOURS	
20 Minutes:	Aloha greeting, Hawaiian Word Match
40 Minutes:	Luau
30 Minutes:	Hawaiian Island I.Q.

ISLAND POPULATION • 10-40 GUESTS

Aloha! Welcome to the beautiful state of Hawaii! Invite your friends to experience the peaceful music, lovely flowers, and delicious food of the Hawaiian Islands. This tropical party is perfect for a casual church fellowship, a neighborhood gathering, or a group of fun-loving friends who enjoy getting together.

Floral Invitations

Send your guests a plastic lei and floral invitation to set the mood for this luau event. Plastic leis are inexpensive and can be found at most party stores. You can also make your own by threading plastic or silk flowers together to create the garland. Attach a small colorful or flowery postcard or stationery note to the lei using ribbon. Send the lei and card in a 6 x 9 brown envelope. The invitation information will read:

ALOHA!
Join us for an evening of
tropical festivities, food, and fun at a

HAWAIIAN LUAU

Date: _____

Time:_____

Hawaiian Island Address: _____

_____

RSVP: _____

(your name and phone number)

Island Decorations

Think tropical! Line the walkway to your front door with tiki torches and/or Chinese lanterns. Place a floral wreath on the door with a sign that says "**Aloha!**" If you want to go the extra mile, create a palm tree effect at your front door using brown mural paper or packaging paper for the trunks. Cut three-foot wide strips about six or seven feet in length. Crumple the paper slightly to give it a realistic 3-D trunk effect and attach to the door using either tape, tacks, or staples. Cut palm branches out of green construction paper. Place a palm tree on both sides of the door.

On a tape or CD player, play Hawaiian music (found at most music stores) as your guests walk in the door and present them with another lei. Use more leis throughout the house along with flowers, pineapples, and coconuts. Inquire at a travel agency concerning posters and brochures that you could use to decorate the walls and tables. Rent a Hawaiian travel video, movie, or episode of *Hawaii Five-0* to play silently on the television. Name tags can be small white cards with fresh or silk flowers attached. Place hibiscus potpourri throughout the house to add a tropical island scent.

Decorate your dining tables with fruits, palm leaves, and florals. At each place setting put a small clear glass bowl with a fresh flower bud floating in water. This may be a good favor for each of your guests to take home if it fits in your budget. Use colorful paper or plastic plates, napkins, and utensils. Bamboo shoots, ukuleles, fish nets with plastic fish, grass skirts, straw hats, and huts are all tremendous ways that you can add to your Hawaiian decor. Find or borrow what you can, but do not go to the trouble to get all of these items. These are simply suggestions to enhance your theme.

Arrival Activities

Aloha Greeting, Hawaiian Word Match

Greet each of your guests in the typical Hawaiian manner, putting a lei around their necks, giving them each a hug (or kiss on the cheek), and saying "Aloha!" [pronounced, ah-Lo-hah].

Take Pictures

Invite guests to have their picture taken with you as they enter. Be sure to get the palm tree in the picture. Designate a "camera buff" friend or hire someone to do the picture taking at the beginning of the party.

Refreshments

Try this fabulous punch recipe:

Barb's Favorite Tropical Punch

1	(46 oz.) can pineapple juice	1 cup lemon juice
1	cup sugar	1 pint cranberry juice
2	quarts ginger ale	cocktail

❖ Chill all ingredients. Combine first four ingredients and stir well. For lively bubbles, add ginger ale at the last minute before guests arrive.

❖ Yields 20 punch cup servings.

Hawaiian Word Match

Hand each guest a piece of paper cut in floral shapes. On half of the flowers, write Hawaiian words (below); on the remaining flowers write the definitions. Some guests will be holding words, while others are holding definitions. Tell your guests that as they mingle with the other guests, they need to try to match the definitions to the words. When they think they have found their match, they are to bring it to you to see if they are correct. You will be holding the master list with the answers. The first couple to discover their match wins a small prize, such as a visor or sunglasses. Here are the words to use for the game. Include the pronunciation with the word.

WORD	PRONUNCIATION	DEFINITION
ala	AH-lah	road
hula	HOO-lah	dance
kai	KAH-i	the sea
kane	KAH-nay	boy or man
kapa	KAH-pah beaten bark	cloth made of
kukui	koo-KOO-i	the candlenut tree
lanai	lah-NAH-i	a porch
lei	LAY-i	a wreath or garland
luau	loo-AH-oo	a feast
mahalo	MAH-hah-lo	thank you
malihini	MAH-li-HI-ni	a newcomer
mauna	mah-OO-nah	mountain
mele	MAY-lay	a song or chant
muumuu	MOO-oo-MOO-oo	a simple gown
nene	Nay-nay	the Hawaiian goose
pali	PAH-li	a cliff
pau	PAH-oo or POW	finished, done
poi	POH-i or POY	food made from taro plant
wahine	wah-HI-nay	a girl or woman

You could also use this information for an after dinner game in which you say a Hawaiian word and participants try to guess the meaning.

Luau Menu

Fruit Splendor
Luau Pork Roast
Tropical Almond Rice
Hawaiian Sweet Bread
Chocolate Macadamia Nut Cake
Ice Cream Coconut Balls

Serve your luau buffet style. You may want to use bamboo trays for your guests to carry their food or decorate tables at which to sit.

Fruit Splendor

2 (20 oz) cans chunk pineapple
1 (11 oz) can mandarin oranges, drained
2 sliced bananas   ½ cup shredded coconut
1 cup mini-marshmallows   ½ cup chopped walnuts (optional)

❖ Gently combine all ingredients including juice from one can of pineapples. Toss lightly.
❖ An empty pineapple shell would make a lovely dish for the presentation of this salad.
❖ Yields 8 servings.

Luau Pork Roast

5 lb boneless pork roast   3 jars strained apricot baby food
½ cup honey   ¼ cup lemon juice
¼ cup soy sauce   1 garlic clove, minced
1 onion, finely chopped   1 cup ginger ale
   dash of pepper

❖ Place roast in a shallow baking dish. Combine all ingredients, reserving one jar of apricots. Pour over roast and marinate in the refrigerator for 4 hours, turning occasionally. Remove pork from marinade (reserving marinade) and place the pork on a spit or kettle-type grill. Cook over low coals for about 3½ hours (or until inserted meat thermometer registers 185°.) During the last ½ hour baste every 10 minutes with the reserved marinade. Five minutes before removing from grill, spread the last jar of apricots over the roast.
❖ Yields 6 servings.

Tropical Almond Rice

1 small clove garlic, minced	2 Tbsp oil
1 cup slivered almonds	
½ medium red or green pepper, cut into strips	
⅛ tsp black pepper	2 cups water
1½ cups white rice	1 Tbsp soy sauce

❖ Saute garlic in oil in skillet until lightly browned. Add red pepper, black pepper, and water. Bring quickly to a boil over high heat. Stir in rice. Lower temperature and cover, allowing to simmer for 20 minutes. Just before serving, add almonds and soy sauce, tossing lightly.

Hawaiian Sweetbread

❖ Many grocery stores carry Hawaiian sweetbread, which comes in round loaves and is usually found in the bakery section of the store.

Chocolate Macadamia Nut Cake

2 cups sugar	2 cups flour
1 stick margarine	4 Tbsp cocoa
½ cup shortening	1 cup water
½ cup buttermilk	1 tsp soda
2 eggs, beaten	1 tsp vanilla

❖ Combine sugar and flour; set aside. Melt margarine, cocoa, shortening, and water, bringing to a boil. Stir in sugar and flour mixture. Add rest of ingredients, mixing well.

❖ Pour into a well-greased 9 x 13 pan and bake at 400° for 20 minutes.

❖ Yields 8–10 servings.

Icing:

1 stick butter	4 Tbsp cocoa
6 Tbsp milk	1 small box powdered sugar
1 tsp vanilla	1 cup macadamia nut pieces

❖ Melt butter. Add milk and cocoa and bring to boil. Remove from heat and add powdered sugar, vanilla, and nuts.

Ice Cream Coconut Balls

❖ Roll balls of vanilla ice cream in grated coconut and serve next to slice of cake. Can be made earlier in the day and kept in the freezer until serving time.

Conversation Booster

Ask your guests to discuss the following question over dinner: "If you were stranded on a deserted island and could choose three items to help you survive, what would they be?"

You may choose to further this discussion after dinner by speaking to the group about our need for God. Psalm 34 is an excellent psalm to read concerning the Lord's care and sufficiency. Other Scriptures include John 4:1–14 and Psalm 103.

After-Dinner Fun and Fellowship

Hawaiian Island I.Q.

Your guests are sure to have a blast as you test their knowledge of the great state of Hawaii. The number of points is based on the difficulty of the question and on every correct answer. Point value is listed after each answer. Provide a simple prize such as coconut cookies, Hawaiian java, or chocolate macadamia nut candies.

Divide into small groups according to the color of lei the guests received when they arrived. Each team will be given a stack of brightly colored paper and a marker. One person on each team will write the team's answers on the paper and hold it up. After you read a question, the teams will have one minute to write their answer. When you give the signal, they are to hold up their answers simultaneously.

Q: Name the seven main islands of Hawaii.
A: Niihau, Kauai, Oahu, Molokai, Lanai, Maui, and Hawaii. (Award five points for each team that gets five of the seven islands correct. Ten points for any team that names all seven islands.)

Q: What is Hawaii's state bird and state flower.

A: Nene (Hawaiian goose) and hibiscus. (Ten points if they get both answers correct, five if they name one.)

Q: Which of the following is the state motto of Hawaii?
    a. Beauty is life
    b. All are one
    c. The life of the land is perpetuated in righteousness
    d. Hang loose

A: c (Ten points)

Q: What is the nickname of the state of Hawaii?

A: "The Aloha State" (Ten points)

Q: Name the first Hawaiian king.

A: King Kamehameha (Ten points)

Q: What are the two chief products of Hawaii?

A: Pineapple and cane sugar (Five points for each correct answer)

Q: Hawaii was visited by a British captain in 1778. What was his name?

A: James Cook. (Ten points for the full name, five points for the last name only)

Q James Cook originally called the islands The
_____ Islands. Fill in the blank.

A: Sandwich Islands (Ten points)

Q: Name the highest peak or the largest volcanic mountain in Hawaii.

A: Mauna Kea, highest peak at 13,796 feet. Mauna Loa, largest volcanic mountain in the world in cubic content at 13,679 feet. (Five points for each)

Q: The Iolani Palace in Hawaii holds national significance. Why?

A: It is the only royal palace in the United States. (Ten points)

Final Note

When I think of Hawaii in all of its splendor, I thank God for His marvelous creation. The beautiful birds, lush landscapes, and even the grand volcanoes are an awesome testimony of His handiwork. When we reflect on this wonderful island paradise, perhaps we get just a touch of what heaven will be like. Oh the majesty and wonder of what He has prepared for us!

> "Come, you blessed of My Father, inherit the kingdom prepared for you from the foundation of the world."
>
> MATTHEW 25:34

Chapter 9

USOLVIT MYSTERY DINNER PARTY

MYSTERY GAME SCHEDULE • 1.5 HOURS

40 minutes:	Arrival, eat, mingle, and play Instruction Tape and News Flash #1
5 Minutes:	News Flash #2
5 Minutes:	Diary is delivered and then read to the group
5 Minutes:	News Flash #3
5 Minutes:	News Flash #4
10 Minutes:	Read appointment book, make phone call to salon, and listen to News Flash #5
5 Minutes:	News Flash #6 and ask everyone to put their pieces of the puzzle (received in the packet) together to discover the final clue.
5 Minutes:	Detectives submit their hypothesis.
10 Minutes:	News Flash #7.

NUMBER OF DETECTIVES • 5–25 GUESTS

Miss Julienne Stone, heiress to the Stone Diamond fortune, is missing! Your guests will act as detectives to help solve the mystery! Through news flashes and a variety of evidence, the detectives will piece together the story of Julienne Stone to figure out where she is, with whom, and why. As the host of this mysterious event, you will prepare the clues given in this chapter and personalize them to your own home town.

Supersleuth Invitations

Your invitations will be in secret code, and the detective invitees must break the code to understand the invitation. Type the invitation information on gray paper. The invitation should read as follows:

You Are Invited to a Mystery Party!

This invitation contains vital information that can be figured out only by an accomplished detective such as yourself.

```
Fkppgt uvctvu cv UGXGP
fcvg:
Cfftguu:
```

Key: For each letter given, think of the letter that comes two places before it in the alphabet. For *A* and *B* move back to *Y* and *Z*. If you still can't figure it out, just call me and I'll tell you all of the party info (__phone number__), but this will make me slightly concerned about your supersleuth skills. Call me anyway just to let me know if you are coming.

The coded part of the invitation says: Dinner starts at seven, Date: _____, Address:_____. For your invitation, write as much of the information as possible in code.

Party Decorations

Start your decorations at the door with an official sign that says, "Usolvit Detective Agency." Use gray and dark green as your main theme colors. For the food table, use dark green cloths, plates, and napkins. A hardback Sherlock Holmes book standing upright with a large magnifying glass leaning against it makes a great centerpiece. If you are able to find a hat similar to Mr. Holmes's, then place it by the book. Set out other mystery books throughout the party area, along with glasses and other funny disguises. Wear a raincoat to greet your guests and play Henry Mancini's "Pink Panther" music.

If possible, put a desk near the door so that when your guests arrive they will walk to the desk where you will enlist their services as a detective. On your desk place several large brown envelopes with "TOP SECRET" written across the front. You should have one envelope for each participant or couple. The envelope will contain the Suspect Checklist, a blank memo pad, a pen, and a puzzle piece (see Pre-Mystery Preparation for details). Inexpensive magnifying glasses or a disguise would be fun to include as well, if budget allows.

The name tags should look like official badges with "USOLVIT DETECTIVE AGENCY" written at the top and DETECTIVE (guest's name) written underneath. Instruct your guests that during the evening they are free to eat and mingle, but they must be very observant. Encourage them to write down every bit of information that they think may be relevant to the case. Tell them that most of their information will come in the form of news flashes so stay tuned!

Pre-Mystery Preparation

This is a copy of the checklist each detective will receive in their Top Secret envelope. You may want to replace some of the location names with the names of places in your own city.

The Mystery of Julienne Stone
Where will she be found?

- At the mall
- At the hair salon
- In Europe
- At a local hotel
- In a nearby town

With Whom?
- The banker: Dave McClutchin
- The doctor: Justin Thyme
- The lawyer: Hugh Dunnit
- The hairdresser: Marcella Mousse
- Her best friend: Faith Fulchum

Why?
- She was kidnapped.
- She eloped.
- She was depressed.
- She was shopping.
- She was ill.

Puzzle Piece

Before the party, you will need to create a puzzle piece for the Top Secret envelope. The puzzle piece will be a part of the evidence used later in the game. Write the following words on a large piece of paper.

> **Dear J.**
>
> **Don't worry! I'll be there as soon as I finish my research.**
>
> **I Love You,**
> **D.**

Crumple up the paper with the note and then cut it into puzzles pieces, being careful to provide one for each person. Put the puzzle piece in the Top Secret envelope along with the rest of the goodies. Your guests may start piecing together the puzzle with the others as they begin to interact. Allow them to do so. If they do not take the initiative to put together the puzzle, then you will find a designated time to work on the puzzle later in the party.

News Flashes and Other Evidence

Before the party day you will need to make preparations for the clue presentations. Throughout the night you will provide significant clues in the form of news flashes and evidence. You will need to decide how you want to convey the news flash announcements. You may choose to read the news flash directly to your guests as if you are a reporter. If possible, before the party takes place, videotape yourself or a friend acting as a news reporter. When it comes time to give a news flash during the party, you simply turn on the prerecorded video for your guests to view the information. You could also tape record a news flash on an audio tape and play it as if it is radio news. Your guests will be both entertained and amused with your creativity and humor.

Since there are seven news flashes, they should be spaced out about every five minutes with other clues revealed in between.

Below you will find the news flashes as well as the other evidence that you will need to prepare.

Detectives Fellowship

Your guests will be eating, mingling, and playing throughout the evening. It is best to provide a buffet of finger food and hors d'oeuvres for dinner so that your guests can walk around with a plate of food and talk to other guests. Use the hors d'oeuvres recipes found in this book (check index) or provide pizzas or sub sandwiches. You could also choose one of the theme parties in chapters 2–10 and adjust this mystery to fit the theme. A Western Mystery, Hawaiian Five-O Detective Game, or Formal Dinner Party Mystery could be fun.

Presenting the Clues

Introduction Tape

Start out the evening with a prerecorded message on tape saying the following:

Welcome to the Usolvit Mystery Party. You have been hired by the Usolvit Detective Agency to piece together the clues of a very important mystery. Diamond heiress Julienne Stone is missing. Your job, should you choose to accept it, is to find out where she is, with whom, and why. Keep alert and be aware of any clues that may be provided throughout the evening. This tape will self-destruct in fifteen seconds.

(Close the tape with music similar to that of the show "Mission Impossible" and make a sizzle sound. I'm still trying to figure out how to make smoke come out of the recorder!)

News Flash #1

Good evening. This is (your name or friend's name), Channel 6, station KLUE news. This information just in. Julienne Stone, twenty-three-year-old daughter of diamond tycoon Jim Stone, has been missing since yesterday afternoon. No one knows her whereabouts, but she was last seen leaving (name of a local mall in or around your area) at approximately 3:30 Thursday afternoon. At this point, no ransom note has been found. Julienne works for the elite accounting firm of Kountit and Chequet. We will keep you up-to-date on the latest findings as they happen. This is _____ with KLUE TV Channel 6.

News Flash #2

Now back to the ongoing investigation concerning Julienne Stone who has been missing since late Thursday afternoon. We are at the home of the Stone's family friend and banker, Dave McClutchin. Mr. McClutchin is offering a $10,000 reward to anyone providing information concerning the whereabouts of Ms. Stone. Mr. McClutchin, who intended to marry Ms. Stone, is very concerned about her safety. He claims that he was supposed to meet Julienne for dinner on Thursday at 6:00, but she never arrived.

He can't imagine who would have taken her, but he

did say that lately she had been acting strangely and a little
aloof. We'll bring you more information as it is revealed.
For now this is _____ with station
KLUE Channel 6 reporting live.

Special Delivery

After the second news flash you will announce that Federal
Parcel Express has just delivered a package. (You can actually
have a co-host go out the back door and ring the front door
bell for delivery.) Inside is a brief note from Jim Stone along
with Julienne's diary. The note should read:

Dear Usolvit Detective Agency:

I am contacting you in hopes that you can help me
find my precious daughter, Julienne. The reward will
be well worth your time. I have sent along Julienne's
diary, as I hope it may help lead you to Julienne.
Please read Wednesday's entry—the day before her
disappearance. Julienne has not been herself ever since
we came back from our trip and I am concerned
about her health and her safety. Thank you for your
top priority concerning this matter and please hurry.

Sincerely,
Jim Stone

Julienne's Diary

You will need to purchase an inexpensive diary or use an old
diary or blank book that you already own. Put Julienne Stone
or J. S. on the cover. Read only Wednesday's entry. It should say
the following:

Wednesday:

Dear Diary,

I can't believe how time flies! Sorry that I
haven't written in several days, but I've been so busy

working and getting settled in again after the trip. The trip with Dad was tremendous. Oh, the sights that we saw! What an interesting place, full of history and tradition. I can't wait to go back. The food was good, but I sure regret drinking the water!

If it hadn't been for Faith's wedding, I would have stayed a little longer, but I could never miss the privilege of being my best bud's maid of honor. Besides, I sure missed D. We had a blast together at the rehearsal dinner and wedding reception! I enjoyed meeting his parents. I hope they liked me as much as I liked them.

I'm so happy for Faith. She was a gorgeous bride, and her wedding was beautiful. Who knows, maybe I'll be next! I'm more in love than I ever thought I could be, but ever since Mother died, Daddy has been protective of me. I hope that Daddy will understand that his little girl is old enough to get married now.

I have not been feeling well lately, and I'm anxious to find out about the blood tests that the hospital ran today. They say that love can do funny things to you, but I feel weak and tired all of the time now. Well, I have a busy day tomorrow, so I better say good-bye.

Love, J. S.

News Flash #3

There has been a big break in the continuing story of missing diamond heiress Julienne Stone. An orderly at (name of hospital in your area) has confirmed that he saw Julienne Stone leave the hospital with a man and a woman Thursday evening around 5:00 P.M. The orderly, Esau Hertu, reports that Ms. Stone was wearing a blue dress and seemed to be in a hurry.

We attempted to interview her doctor, Justin Thyme, but he was not available for comment. Stay tuned as we continue to bring you "on the spot" reports of this mysterious disappearance.

News Flash #4

We are here at the home of Fred and Frieda Fulchum, parents of socialite and recently married Faith Fulchum Numore. Faith, who is Julienne's best friend, is out of the country on her honeymoon. Her parents talked with her this morning concerning the mysterious disappearance. According to her parents, Faith stated that although Julienne was impulsive at times, she can't imagine that she would just disappear out of the blue. Faith was determined to return early from her honeymoon, but her parents suggested that she wait for further details before making a decision to return home.

Faith's parents mentioned that they have known Julienne since she was a little girl and do not know of anyone who would want to harm her. They stated that Faith had recently mentioned someone has been bothering Julienne in the past few months. The Fulchums have reported this information to the FBI and to lawyer, Hugh Dunnit.

Mr. Dunnit, the family lawyer for more than twenty years, is presently in Europe on business and cannot be reached for questioning. We will continue to report it as we hear it. For now, this is _____
with station KLUE Channel 6.

Julienne's Appointment Book

Next, you will need to fill in three pages of an appointment book. Use an old daily appointment book or simply make pages that look as if they are from an appointment book. Again, put Julienne's name or initials on the cover. Attach a short handwritten note from Jim Stone saying that he found this evidence and wants you to pay close attention to Wednesday through Friday's entries. You need only read these three days of entries to your guests. Julienne's appointment book should show the following:

Wednesday:

8:00   Work
12:00   Lunch break and appointment for blood work
4:00   Library (travel books)
5:00   Brakes checked on car
6:00   Dinner with dad

Thursday:

8:00   Work (Audit at Dunnit and Didnott)
3:00   Drop off gift exchanges for Faith
4:00   Stop by D.'s
5:00   Hair appointment, Marcella 459-3421
6:00   Dinner with Dave

Friday:

8:00   Work (Wrap up audit at D & D)
10:00   Conference call with Hugh (Europe)
3:30   Airport (Faith and Frank)

Phone Call with Hairdresser

After reading Julienne's schedule, hopefully someone will say that we should call the hair salon to see if she made her appointment. If no one says anything, you may want to draw attention to the phone number, by saying, "Look they even gave a phone number!" Pretend to dial the phone to call the salon, then turn on the tape recorder as if to let all of the guests listen on speaker phone. You may even want to record the sounds of the dialing of the phone. Disguise your voice for the recording of Marcella or record someone else's voice saying the following:

Marcella: *Hello, Betty's Beautiful Hair Salon. This is Marcella Mousse, how may I help you?*

You say: *Yes, this is* _____ *from Usolvit Detective Agency. I just have a quick question. Did Julienne Stone show up for her 5:00 hair appointment on Thursday afternoon?*

Marcella: *Well, let me see. Why, as a matter of fact, she didn't. I was supposed to cut and style her hair as usual. Hey, I heard on the news that they are looking for her. Do you have any clues?*

You say: *Well, yes, just a few.*

Marcella: *Well, let me tell you what I think. You should check out that banker guy she's been seeing: What's-his-name McClutchin. He's a little too aggressive in my opinion. If you ask me, Julienne would be smart to pursue that Hugh fellow. I know he's older, but he sure is handsome. I told her if she doesn't want him, I'll take him. 'Course there are a lot of guys that have their eye on Julienne. She's going to have to find a rich one to keep up with her spending.*

I sure hope nothing happened to Julienne, because she was supposed to help me with my accounting work on Saturday. She helps me balance my books every month. I guess she considers me her charity case! She sure is a sweetheart although she hasn't been the same since her mom died. Well, let me know if I can help you with the investigation.

You say: *Thank you for your time, Ms. Mousse, you have been most helpful.*

Marcella: *Sure, anytime. Bye now.*

News Flash #5

Just in over the wire, a major breakthrough on the Julienne Stone case. FBI officials have just confirmed that a hidden camera video at the (name of local pharmacy) has discovered videotape of Ms. Stone at the store on Thursday evening. Sources say that the video shows Ms. Stone getting a prescription and is accompanied by a woman. The pharmacy has confirmed that the drug Dozelot, for which Julienne was getting a prescription filled, is usually used to fight the deadly Shurtadi infection. Our medical correspondent tells us that this illness is only contracted from the drinking water in certain foreign countries. He stated that Dozelot is also used for treatment of migraines, motion sickness, water retention, and certain emotional conditions. We will keep you informed on the latest developments. As for now, this is _____ with KLUE, Channel 6.

News Flash #6

Important new information has just been released concerning the disappearance of Miss Julienne Stone, diamond heiress. Local police have just confirmed that Ms. Stone's 1996 white BMW has been found in a remote parking lot of the (name of local hospital). Everything seems to be intact and there is no evidence of foul play. Slips of paper, perhaps from an important note, were also found at the scene and delivered to the Usolvit Detective Agency for investigation. Detectives are now piecing together the clues to hopefully reveal the whereabouts of Ms. Stone. More information to you as we have it. This is _____ _____ from KLUE, Channel 6.

Mystery Note

Now it is time to piece together the puzzle if your guests have not already done so. Once the puzzle note has been read, it is time for every detective to make their hypothesis as to the whereabouts of Ms. Stone, with whom and why. Give your guests a few moments to deliberate before the last news flash is presented and reveals all. Tell each participant to use the suspect list that they received in their packets and circle their guesses (one in each category), putting their name at the top of the paper. Detectives may work in pairs if you so desire. Once all of the suspect lists have been confiscated, present the final news flash.

News Flash #7

This is _____ from KLUE Channel 6. A happy ending to a near tragedy! Miss Julienne Stone, missing since Thursday evening has been found! She is in good condition, and sources say that friends and family are much relieved to have her home. Here with us now is our roving reporter, _____ explaining the details.

Well _____, apparently Thursday afternoon Julienne stopped by the hospital to find out the results of her blood work done late Wednesday. It was then that she found out that she had picked up the rare and deadly Shurtadi virus. Upon learning of her rare sickness and imminent death, she became distraught. Julienne's doctor and apparent boyfriend, Justin Thyme, M.D. (whom Julienne calls Doc), called his parents to assist Julienne in going to a hospital in their nearby town. Julienne, not wanting to prematurely upset her dad, chose not to inform him of her illness at this point.

Being a prominent figure in her own town, Julienne wanted to be in a place where she would not be easily recognized. As she left, Justin handed her a brief note assuring her that he would stay at the hospital to research possible cures or solutions to this dreaded disease. Thinking there was no hope, she tore up the note and left it in her car when she went to move her car to long-term parking.

After leaving the hospital late Thursday, Justin's parents took Julienne to get her prescription filled. The medicine made her drowsy, so Justin's parents took her on to the hospital and checked her into a room. She remained in her hospital room in a sleepy state with Mr. and Mrs. Thyme keeping a bedside vigil until Justin arrived on Friday. He stayed up all night studying medical cases at the local university library. He had studied the medical cases relating to this dreaded disease and found that in some cases a misdiagnosis can be made. The Shurtadi disease tests very similarly to the Gunnaliv disease.

While at the hospital, they retested and found that she had the treatable Gunnaliv disease.

As they were rejoicing, they turned on the television in the hospital room and discovered that a major search was going on for Julienne. Justin's parents quickly called authorities and put to rest the mystery.

To recap, Julienne Stone has been found in a nearby town, at the hospital, with Dr. Justin Thyme at her bedside. As for Dave McClutchin, the poor soul couldn't bear losing Julienne to the handsome doctor, so he called her continuously. She finally decided to meet him for dinner to tell him that there was no hope for them and that she was in love with Justin. Speaking of Justin, the fear of losing her made him more determined than ever to marry Julienne. When he brought the good medical report he also brought a proposal of marriage.

Final Note

Do not be discouraged if no one is able to guess all three answers correctly (in most mystery parties it is rare for someone to figure out the exact answer). Award a prize to the person or couple who is closest to the correct solution.

For prizes and/or favors consider note pads and pens, sunglasses or funny nose disguises, inexpensive magnifying glasses and/or a small paperback mystery novel. If you are planning to use a favor bag, put the favors in brown paper lunch sacks and write **TOP SECRET** on the sides.

You can read about a great mystery described by Paul in the Bible:

> Behold, I tell you a mystery: We shall not all sleep, but we shall all be changed—in a moment, in the twinkling of an eye, at the last trumpet.
>
> 1 CORINTHIANS 15:51–52.

Perhaps in our lifetime, we as Christians will participate in this incredible mystery of the rapture. Are you ready?

Chapter 10

FORMAL DINNER WITH CLASS

SOPHISTICATED SCHEDULE • 1.5–2 HOURS	
30 Minutes:	Greet, chat, and enjoy hors d'oeuvres
60 Minutes:	Fine Dining
30 Minutes:	Quotable Quotes (if guests stay at your house)

TABLE • 4–8 GUESTS

Experience a formal evening of culture and sophistication at the finest restaurant in town—Your Place! Guests will enjoy an elegant dinner served by an exceptional staff. This is the perfect dinner party to be coupled with a night at the symphony, the opera, a museum, or a round of the intellectually stimulating game, "Quotable Quotes," included in this chapter.

Formal Invitations

Calligraphy or formal print on fine stationery or parchment paper will create a elegant invitation for your guests. Your information should read:

_The honor of your
presence is requested
for dinner at the home of_

your name
your address
Seating time: _____
Date: (write out day and date, no abbreviations)
Semi-Formal Attire
RSVP: _____

Elegant Decorations

This party provides a marvelous opportunity to bring out your best china, silver, and serving dishes that you have hidden away to be used for only "special occasions."

I suggest that you attempt to seat all of your guests at the same table. Use white tablecloths and napkins. Fold the napkins in fans as described in chapter 1. Place a fresh flower arrangement at the center of your table with candlesticks on both sides. Don't forget to light the candles when dinner begins.

Dim the lights for this occasion and play soft classical music by Bach, Mozart, or Beethoven. Add to the ambiance by using potpourri or scented candles.

For this event the decorations are minimal and will cost you very little. An added extra that can make this party special is to hire one or two helpers or servers who can assist in serving the food while you are seated with your guests. This does not need to be expensive. High school students, off-duty waitresses or waiters, relatives, or friends may be possibilities. Pay your staff a fair price. The helpers will have a wonderful time as well. Ask the waiter to wear a suit (or tuxedo if he has one), and the waitress to wear a black dress with a white ruffle apron.

If you know a talented pianist, harpist, or violinist, you may want to see if he or she could perform a short segment for your guests either before, during, or after dinner. A talented college student who is willing to play for a small fee would be a great find.

Arrival Activities

Greet your guests at the door with a warm welcome or allow one of your hired helpers to greet. Since this is a smaller group, invite your guests to sit in the living room or drawing room to chat and enjoy hors d'oeuvres. Prepare simple finger hors d'oeuvres using the recipes below and offer punch to drink.

Hors d'oeuvres

Onion Cheese Puffs

1 envelope onion soup mix   ¼ cup butter or margarine
1 (8 oz) can refrigerator biscuits
  Parmesan cheese

❖ Slice each biscuit into 4 sections. In saucepan melt butter. Over very low heat stir in onion soup mix. Add biscuit pieces and stir gently. Place biscuits on a cookie sheet; bake 5 minutes. Roll baked puffs in Parmesan cheese before serving. Serve hot.
❖ Yields 40 puffs.

Stuffed Mushrooms

1 lb medium-sized mushrooms
1 pkg (10 oz) frozen spinach, defrosted and completely drained
½ cup herb-seasoned stuffing
⅓ cup grated Parmesan cheese
⅓ cup finely chopped green onions
⅓ cup ricotta cheese   1 Tbsp lemon juice

❖ Prepare washed mushrooms by cutting out the stems and brushing them inside and out with melted butter. Stir together the rest of the ingredients until mixture is blended. Scoop mixture into mushroom caps and sprinkle tops lightly with additional grated Parmesan.
❖ Carefully place mushrooms on a lightly greased cookie sheet and bake at 350° for 15–20 minutes. Place under the broiler for a few seconds to brown. Serve at once.
❖ Mushrooms can be assembled earlier in the day and refrigerated before baking.
❖ Yields 25–30 mushrooms.

White Grape Juice Punch

12 large fresh strawberries
 1 (6 oz) can frozen white grape juice
 1 (2 liter) bottle lemon-lime soda, chilled

❖ Wash strawberries and place in freezer overnight. Pour thawed grape juice into punch bowl or large pitcher. Slowly add soda; stir. Add strawberries as garnish to punch bowl or punch cups.

❖ Yields 8–10 servings.

Conversation Booster

Prepare slips of paper with the following questions on them and put them in a goblet or glass bowl. You will need one per guest. Ask your guests to pull a question and tell their answer to the group. This conversation booster can be done during dinner or as you enjoy hors d'oeuvres.

- What book have you read in the past five years that has had an impact on your life?

- If you could have invited anyone in the world to come and speak to our dinner party tonight, whom would you have invited?

- In what area would you say you have an ability or talent?

- If you could spend an evening alone with a good book, what type of book would it be?

- Where is one place in the world that you have never been but would like to visit?

- If you could choose to have one gift, talent, or ability that you do not already possess, what would it be?

- Describe your idea of a perfect vacation.

- What is your favorite type of music and when did you first discover it?

Fine Dining Menu

Once everyone has arrived and had the opportunity to mingle, make the announcement (or let your staff make the announcement) that dinner is served. You will have prepared most of the meal ahead of time so that you can enjoy your guests. Properly instruct your helpers before the party how to heat and maintain the food and how to present it on the plate.

You may want to print a menu with the guest's name at the top and place it on each plate. This also serves as a place card. You will need to put simple yet elegant place cards at each setting if you do not use the menus. Your menu can read as follows:

La Maison De (your name)
welcomes (your guest's name)
(date)

~Shrimp Cocktail~
~Mixed Green Salad~
with blue cheese or basil vinaigrette dressing

~Veal Piccata~
served on a bed of wild rice
with asparagus spears and
steamed baby carrots

~Cream Brulée with Raspberry Topping~

Shrimp Cocktail

1½ lbs medium shrimp, cooked and chilled

❖ Purchase fresh shrimp at your grocery and ask them to boil the shrimp at the store in order to avoid a fishy smell at home. Most fish and meat departments offer this free service. Present shrimp artfully placed on the rim of individual serving bowls, with cocktail sauce in the bowl. Add a slice of lemon to the rim of the bowl as well.

❖ Combine horseradish and ketchup (to taste) to create a wonderful homemade cocktail sauce to your liking or purchase bottled cocktail sauce.

Mixed Green Salad and Dressings

mixed green lettuce   tomato wedges or miniatures
1 cucumber, thinly sliced

❖ Serve on salad plates with choice of dressings offered in
  small pitchers or gravy boats.

Blue Cheese Dressing
2 cups mayonnaise   ½ tsp dry mustard
½ cup dairy sour cream   ½ tsp garlic powder
¼ cup vinegar   ½ tsp onion powder
4 tsp sugar   4 oz blue cheese, crumbled

❖ Mix first seven ingredients; stir in cheese. Cover; refrigerate
  at least 2 hours. Keeps well in refrigerator for two to three
  weeks.
❖ Yields approximately 3 cups.

Basil Vinaigrette Dressing
1 Tbsp Dijon mustard   2 Tbsp lemon juice
2 Tbsp vinegar   6 Tbsp olive oil
6 Tbsp salad oil   salt and pepper
2 Tbsp chopped fresh basil

❖ Beat all ingredients for one minute using a wire whisk.

Veal Piccata

12 slices of veal, scallopini cut   2 Tbsp garlic salt
1 cup water with 4 tsp beef bouillon
1 cup flour   4 Tbsp fresh lemon juice

❖ Dredge veal in garlic salt mixed with flour. Brown in skillet
  with melted butter. Add the water with bouillon and lemon
  juice. Put into a baking dish and bake at 350° for 35 minutes.
  Serve on a bed of wild rice with twisted lemon peel on top.

From the kitchen of Carol Potts, Dallas, Texas

Wild Rice

1 (6 oz) pkg wild rice   chicken broth
½ cup slivered almonds, sautéed in butter

❖ Prepare wild rice according to directions using chicken
  broth instead of water. Add almonds and toss lightly.

Vegetables

- ❖ Asparagus: Steam asparagus until just tender and bright in color. Melt butter and drizzle over asparagus spears.
- ❖ Carrots: Steam carrots until tender; place in serving bowl and mix with 1½ Tbsp freshly squeezed orange juice.

Cream Brulée with Raspberry Topping

1 pint whipping cream	7 egg yolks
1 tsp vanilla	⅛ tsp salt
1 cup brown sugar, firmly packed	

- ❖ Scald cream in top of double boiler. Beat egg yolks until light colored and thick; add vanilla, salt, and ⅓ cup of brown sugar. Add the scalded cream. Return to double boiler and cook over hot water until smooth and about the consistency of thin mayonnaise. Stir constantly so that it will be smooth, and do not overcook or it may curdle. Pour into 4 small, oven-safe bowls. Chill thoroughly.
- ❖ Two hours before serving, sift the remaining brown sugar in an even layer over the top of each bowl of brulée. You may want to use a spatula and press the sugar through a strainer. You should have an even layer of brown sugar about ¼ inch thick.
- ❖ Put bowls under a preheated broiler and watch carefully until the sugar melts in an even glaze. It takes just a few seconds. Chill the dessert once again. Just before serving, drizzle raspberry sauce over the top of the brulée.

Raspberry topping:
- 1 (10 oz) pkg frozen raspberries, thawed
- 1 Tbsp cornstarch

- ❖ Puree thawed raspberries in blender and strain to remove the seeds. Combine with cornstarch and cook over medium heat until slightly thickened. Cool and serve over brulée.

Offer both caffeinated and decaffeinated coffees with dessert.

After-Dinner Fellowship

This dinner party is perfectly suited to be the precursor to an event such as the symphony, the opera, a play, or an art exhibit. If you decide to stay at your place after dinner, enjoy a stimulating game of "Quotable Quotes."

Quotable Quotes

The object of this game is to determine who said what. Read one of the quotes from the list below and let your guests try to decide who said it. (All quotes are referenced from *America's God and Country Encyclopedia of Quotations,* William J. Federer, Fame Publishing, Inc., Coppell, Texas, 1994.) This game is best played in teams or couples to pool the participants' knowledge of history and literature. If the players are stumped and need some hints, help them out by revealing the quoter's occupation or when he or she lived. Teams may guess as many times as they like. Five points will be awarded to the first team to name the correct quoted person. Keep a tally of points and award the winners with a small prize of a rose or a box of chocolates.

Q: "England has two books, the Bible and Shakespeare. England made Shakespeare, but the Bible made England."

A: Victor Marie Hugo (1802–85), French author

Q: "The secret of my success? It is simple. It is found in the Bible, 'In all thy ways acknowledge Him and He shall direct thy paths.'"

A: George Washington Carver (1864–1943), agricultural chemist

Q: "I have been driven many times upon my knees by the overwhelming conviction that I had nowhere else to go. My own wisdom, and that of all about me, seemed insufficient for that day."

A: Abraham Lincoln (1809–65), sixteenth president of United States

Q: "Oh God, let this horrible war quickly come to an end that we may all return home and engage in the only work that is worthwhile—and that is the salvation of men."

A: Thomas Jonathan "Stonewall" Jackson (1824–63), one of the country's great generals

Q: "I am trying to prevent anyone from saying the really foolish thing that people often say about Him: 'I am ready to accept Jesus as a great moral teacher, but I don't accept His claims to be God.' That is one thing we must not say.

"A man who was merely a man and said the sort of things that Jesus said would not be a great moral teacher. He would either be a lunatic on a level with the man who says he is a poached egg—or else he would be the devil of hell.

"You must make your choice. Either this man was, and is, the Son of God: or else a madman or something worse."

A: C. S. Lewis (1898–1963), professor (Oxford and Cambridge), renowned English novelist

Q: "The hand of Providence has been so conspicuous in all this [the course of the war] that he must be worse than an infidel that lacks faith, and more wicked that has not gratitude to acknowledge his obligations; but it will be time enough for me to turn Preacher when my present appointment ceases."

A: George Washington (1732-99), first president of United States

Q: "The Bible is no mere book, but a Living Creature, with a power that conquers all that oppose it."

A: Napoleon Bonaparte I (1769–1821), Emperor of France

Q: "God helps them that help themselves."

A: Benjamin Franklin (1706-90), statesman, author, scientist, printer, diplomat, governor, founder of University of Pennsylvania

Q: "Twant me,'twas the Lord. I always told Him, 'I trust to You. I don't know where to go or what to do, but I expect You to lead me,' and He always did."

A: Harriet Tubman (1821-1913), former slave who repeatedly risked her life to free over 300 slaves

Q: "How can anyone lose who chooses to become a Christian? If, when he dies, there turns out to be no God and his faith was in vain, he has lost nothing—in fact, he has been happier in life than his nonbelieving friends. If, however, there is a God and a heaven and hell, then he has gained heaven and his skeptical friends will have lost everything in hell."

A: Blaise Pascal (1623–62), renowned scientist and mathematician

Q: "My hope in the One who created us all sustains me: He is an ever present help in trouble. . . . When I was extremely depressed, He raised me with His right hand, saying, 'O man of little faith, get up, it is I; do not be afraid.'"

A: Christopher Columbus (1451–1506), mapmaker, voyager, discoverer

Q: "Soldiers! Let us humble ourselves before the Lord, our God, asking through Christ, the forgiveness of our sins, beseeching the aid of the God of our forefathers in the defense of our homes and our liberties, thanking Him for His past blessings, and imploring their continuance upon our cause and our people."

A: Robert E. Lee (1807–70), general of the Confederate Army

Q: "If the Ten Commandments were not written by Moses, then they were written by another fellow of the same name."

A: Mark Twain (1835–1910), author

Q: "I shall allow no man to belittle my soul by making me hate him."

A: Booker T. Washington (1856–1915), great American reformer, educator, and writer

Q: "When I think of my God, my heart dances within me for joy, and then my music has to dance, too."

A: Franz Joseph Haydn (1732–1809), Austrian musical composer

Q: "Grow old along with me. The best is yet to be; the last of life, for which the first was made. Our times are in His hands who saith, 'A whole I planned, youth shows but half.' Trust God; see all, nor be afraid."

A: Robert Browning (1812–89), English poet

Q: "If there is anything in my thoughts or style to commend, the credit is due to my parents for instilling in me an early love of the Scriptures. If we abide by the principles taught in the Bible, our country will go on prospering and to prosper; but if we and our posterity neglect its instructions and authority, no man can tell how sudden a catastrophe may overwhelm us and bury all our glory in profound obscurity."

A: Daniel Webster (1782–1852), American politician and diplomat

Q: "The Ten Commandments and the teachings of Jesus are not only basic but plenary."

A: William Holmes McGuffey (1800–73), American educator, author of *McGuffey's Readers*

Q: "I thank God for my handicaps, for, through them, I have found myself, my work, and my God."

A: Helen Keller (1880–1968), American author, lecturer who overcame the tremendous obstacles of being both blind and deaf

Q: "The aim and final end of all music should be none other than the glory of God and the refreshment of the soul. If heed is not paid to this, it is not true music but a diabolical bawling and twanging."

A: Johann Sebastian Bach (1685–1750), German musical composer, considered the "master of the masters"

Q: "Education is useless without the Bible."
A: Noah Webster (1758–1843), statesman, educator, author of *Webster's Dictionary*

Q: "Science brings man nearer to God."
A: Louis Pasteur (1822–95), microbiologist, developed process of milk pasteurization and germ theory of disease

Final Note

Isn't it wonderful?! So many great leaders, famous scientists, and talented individuals had such a deep respect for God. It is important to tell and retell the quotes of these marvelous individuals. Play the "Quotable Quotes" game on trips, over family dinners, and at other gatherings. My hope is that this game will be a faith-building activity for you, your family, and friends.

> How does a man become wise? The first step is to trust and reverence the Lord!
> Proverbs 1: 7 (TLB)

EVENT PARTIES

Rejoice with those who rejoice.

ROMANS 12:15

Chapter 11

WONDERFUL WEDDING SHOWERS

20–30 Minutes: Arrival, punch, and mingling
45 Minutes: Eat and open presents
30–40 Minutes: Shower games

The blissful couple is getting married and you have offered to give one of the showers! Wedding showers are not only a happy celebration, but a special opportunity to bring gifts and encouragement to the wedding couple. Give a gift of love and hospitality by preparing a meaningful event for either the bride-to-be or the couple together. Choose from a variety of recipes and ideas for a bridal shower, as well as some fun and unique ideas for a couples shower.

Bridal Showers

Preferable times for bridal showers are Saturdays—mid-morning, mid-day, or afternoon—or Sunday afternoon. The number of people on the guest list will influence the choice of location. If there are several people giving the shower, then select the home that is best suited for the amount of people involved.

Who Should Host?

Generally the host or hostess is a close friend of either the bride and groom or their parents. A hostess may also be an aunt or a cousin. It is not considered proper for the guest of honor's immediate family to provide a shower (sister, mother, mother-in-law, or daughter).

Themes and Invitations

When you first decide to give a shower for the bride-to-be, ask her what kind of shower she would like to receive. Below you will find several themes for showers, correlating invitations, and the type of guests for which they are best suited. The bride will need to give you an invitation list in plenty of time to prepare the invitations. Send the invitations two weeks in advance and enclose a map. Always include the wedding party and mothers of the bride and groom in the invitation list.

Miscellaneous: general gifts usually from registries. Invite parents' or inlaws' friends or a wide mix of friends and family. Suggested Invitation: Use floral stationery or fine card-stock that coordinates with the colors in the wedding. Tie a ribbon or lace bow around the invitation before putting it in the envelope.

Kitchen: kitchen utensils, pots, pans, dishes, linens, and small appliances. Usually best to invite friends and co-workers. Not a necessary shower for someone who has been on her own for awhile and already has a stocked kitchen. Suggested invitation: Recipe card with shower information; include a blank recipe card for each guest to bring a recipe from their kitchen for the bride-to-be. Collect recipes at party and give to bride in a cute recipe book or box.

Lingerie: nighties, undergarments, robes, slips, and slippers. This shower is best suited for good friends of the bride. Suggested invitation: Use pastel pink paper, printing the invitation information in the center. Glue a strip of white lace trim to the top and the bottom of the paper.

Around the Clock: items that are used at different times around the clock (fully explained for the couple's shower later in this chapter). Invite a wide range of family and friends.

Suggested invitation: Clock face with hands indicating the time of day for which the guest buys a gift. Party information included on the back of the clock.

General wording for a bridal invitation is:

> *Please join us for a (specify type) Bridal Shower*
> *honoring Miss (full name of bride-to-be)*

Time:_____

Date: _____

Address: _____

Add: "Bride-elect of (groom's name)" if many of the guests are friends of the groom's family.

Bridal Decor

Decorate for bridal showers using white netting fabric, bows that match the wedding colors, fresh florals, white balloons, and bells. Carry out your chosen party theme with your decorations as well. For the front door, wrap a Styrofoam wreath in netting material and decorate with bows and flowers that coordinate with the wedding colors. Music should either be wedding music or romantic melodies.

Arrival Activities

Have one of the hostesses greet guests at the door while the bride-to-be stands close by to help introduce her guests to others.

Give each guest a name tag and offer punch or coffee. You can use lovely store-bought name tags (it is easy to find name tags that have a bridal theme), or make your own by cutting white bells out of card-stock paper. Use a bell-shaped cookie cutter to guide you. Other ideas include using doilies, netting, lace, or artificial flowers attached to a plain white name tag. It may be nice for guests to not only put their name, but how they know or are related to the bride-to-be. This also helps to encourage conversation as the guests are mingling.

Ice Cream Citrus Punch

2 (5 or 6 oz cans) frozen lemonade concentrate
1 (6 oz can) frozen orange juice
5 pints pineapple sherbet   1 quart vanilla ice cream

❖ Combine lemonade and orange juice concentrates with 9 cups of cold water. Place sherbet and ice cream in the bottom of a large punch bowl, breaking in small pieces with large spoon. Add juices and stir until sherbet and ice cream are partially melted.
❖ Yields 20 servings.

When most of the guests have arrived, encourage them to get a plate of food and be seated. Before the party, decide with your co-hostess if you want to serve food buffet-style or if you want to prepare the plates beforehand and have the guests simply take a plate and sit down. Generally guests are not seated at tables so keep the foods simple and easy to manage. I usually set chairs in a large circle for the guests. The bride-to-be should be served first so that she can begin unwrapping presents as people are still eating.

Bridal Shower Menu

Strawberries with Dip
Heart-Shaped Chicken Salad Sandwiches
Artichoke Cheese Delights
Wonderful Wedding Shower Tarts

Strawberries with Dip

strawberries, about 4–5 per guest
1 cup sour cream   3 Tbsp brown sugar
dash of poppy seeds

❖ Combine sour cream and brown sugar until blended. Add poppy seeds and serve in a small bowl among strawberries.

Heart-Shaped Chicken Salad Sandwiches

4 cups cooked chicken, shredded
2 cups celery, thinly sliced   ½ Tbsp onion, minced

1 Tbsp lemon juice	¾ cup mayonnaise
¼ cup whipping cream	salt and pepper

❖ Combine chicken and celery and toss gently. Mix next four ingredients and add to chicken until coated. Season with salt and pepper and spread on wheat or white bread. Use heart-shaped cookie cutters to cut the sandwiches and arrange creatively on serving plates.

❖ Yields 20–24 finger sandwiches.

Artichoke Cheese Delights

1 (14 oz) can artichoke hearts	
1 cup seasoned bread crumbs	2 Tbsp olive oil
1 Tbsp lemon juice	2 Tbsp Parmesan cheese
2 eggs	2 garlic cloves, crushed
(extra bread crumbs and cheese for rolling)	

❖ Drain and chop artichoke hearts. Combine all ingredients and roll into 1-inch balls. Roll the balls in the extra bread crumbs and Parmesan cheese. Bake in 350° oven for 15 minutes. Balls can be made ahead of time and frozen before being baked. When ready to use, simply thaw to room temperature and cook according to directions.

❖ Yields 24 bite-size servings.

Wonderful Wedding Shower Tarts

1¼ cups all-purpose flour	½ cup butter, room temperature
3 Tbsp sugar	½ tsp vanilla extract
¼ cup finely chopped pecans	
25 Two-inch miniature fluted tart pans	
(available at cookware shops)	

❖ In a medium bowl, combine flour, butter, sugar, vanilla, and pecans. Blend with a fork until mixture resembles fine crumbs. Knead until dough holds together. Press a scant tablespoon of dough into bottom and up sides of each tart pan (ungreased). Place tart pans one inch apart on baking sheets. Bake 10–11 minutes or until lightly golden. Cool slightly in pans; then with the point of a sharp knife loosen edges to release tarts from pans. Cool on racks. Just before serving, fill with a little cream cheese filling and top with kiwi or strawberry slices.

Cream Cheese Filling

1 (3 oz) pkg of cream cheese	1 Tbsp whipping cream or milk
2 Tbsp powdered sugar	½ tsp vanilla extract

❖ In a small bowl beat together the ingredients until smooth
❖ Yields 25 tarts.

NOTE: For a brunch menu, use the delicious quiche recipe found in chapter 12.

Open Presents

After most people have finished eating, the honoree can begin opening presents. Assign one hostess to write down the gifts and the giver's name and another hostess to help with the wrapping paper and gifts. Pass around the gifts as they are opened so the guests can see the presents, and display them nicely on a nearby table. Collect all of the bows and staple them to a paper plate. This makes a creative bouquet for the bride to use at the wedding rehearsal. After the gifts have been opened, it is always nice to hear from the honoree. First, allow her to say thank you to the group as a whole and then ask her to share a little information about her fiancé. Most people love to hear the story of how the couple met and what their plans are for the honeymoon and life after the honeymoon.

An added activity that is both meaningful and lasting is to have each guest write a bit of wise wedding or marriage advice for the bride-to-be. Each guest may want to write something that she once heard or something that has been helpful in her own experience or even a Bible verse. Provide pens and pretty paper for each participant. You may want to use paper cut in the shape of hearts or wedding bells. Put the advice in a photo album for a special keepsake along with pictures from the shower.

Bridal Shower Games

Games can be enjoyable and entertaining but are not a necessity for a successful shower. Here are some fantastic shower favorites to consider:

Loving Nicknames. Provide colorful paper and pencils for your guests and ask them to make a list of commonly used nicknames for spouses. Names such as "Honey," "Buttercup," or "Sweetie Pie." Tell the participants that they have one minute to write down as many nicknames as they can think of. Give a prize (such as chocolates or a flower) to the person who has the most nicknames listed. Next, ask the winner to read her list and give everyone a chance to try to define the nickname and how it is used. Example: "Honey" is used when you are about to tell your spouse that you put a dent in the car. "Buttercup" is used when you are going to ask your husband to do a chore or favor.

Anniversary Years. Using a white poster board decorated with white lace, write the numbers that you see below down the left side of the poster. The players will try to guess all of the types of anniversary gifts that go with the year of marriage. Encourage your guests to work together as a group. Once everyone thinks that the list is correct, then check it with the one listed here. No prizes with this game, just the fun of working together!

Anniversaries

YEAR	TYPE	YEAR	TYPE
1.	Paper	13.	Lace
2.	Cotton	14.	Ivory
3.	Leather	15.	Crystal
4.	Books, fruit, or flowers	20.	China
5.	Wood or clocks	25.	Silver
6.	Iron or candy	30.	Pearl
7.	Copper, bronze, brass, or wool	35.	Jade or coral
8.	Electrical appliances	40.	Ruby
9.	Pottery or willow	45.	Sapphire
10.	Tin or aluminum	50.	Gold
11.	Steel	55.	Emerald
12.	Silk or linen	60.	Diamond
		75.	Diamond

Wisdom from Above. Read the first few words of a proverb and ask your guests to finish the phrase. You will have loads of fun as you attempt to finish sayings. To make the game more humorous, before the party tape-record the groom reading the first words of the proverb, then stop the tape to let the ladies finish the thought. Read the correct ending after several people have attempted to answer. Translations may vary.

A wise woman /
> *builds her home.*

Charm is deceitful and beauty is vain /
> *but a woman who fears God,*
> *she shall be praised.*

Love covers /
> *a multitude of sins.*

What God hath joined together /
> *let no man put asunder.*

Therefore shall a man leave his mother and father /
> *and cleave unto his wife.*

And now abide faith, hope, love, these three /
> *but the greatest of these is love.*

A soft answer /
> *turns away anger.*

He who finds a wife /
> *finds a good thing.*

A prudent wife is /
> *from the Lord.*

Couples Shower

A couples shower is a wonderful opportunity to invite friends of both the bride and the groom. The best time for this event is usually a weekend night for dinner. A hamburger cookout, western buffet (see Western party, chap. 7), Mexican food (chap. 13), or sub sandwiches could all be possible menu ideas for this event. It helps to have a theme for your party. Here are two ideas from which to choose.

Themes and Invitation

Home Improvement Shower. Invite your guests to join you for a little tool time. On the invitation ask the guests to bring tools that the bride and groom can use around the house, yard, or even kitchen. Invitations can be in the shape of a house, or you may want to attach the invitation to small plastic toy tool and mail in a large brown envelope. The information should read as follows:

IT'S A HOME IMPROVEMENT SHOWER
FOR (COUPLE'S NAMES)

Join us for dinner and some tool time fun on

Date: _____

Time:_____

Address: _____

Please bring a tool to help the new couple
in the house, yard, garden, or kitchen.

RSVP: _____

As the host or hostess of the event you may want to provide a new tool box and a large basket in which to place the gifts.

Around the Clock Shower. Each guest will be given a different time of the day on their invitation and will bring a gift to be used during that time. For instance, if the given time is 7:00 A.M., it is generally assumed that breakfast takes place during this time, so the guest may bring a coffee maker or a waffle iron as a gift.

The invitation will look like a clock face on one side and the party information is written on the other. On the clock face, draw hands showing the designated time for which the gift should be bought. Put A.M. or P.M. on the clock face as well. The information on the back should read as follows:

AROUND THE CLOCK

(couple's name)

could use our help!
Please join us to honor the wedding couple.
We ask that you bring a gift that could be used
at the designated time on the clock
found on the back of this invitation.

Party time: _____

Date: _____

Address: _____

RSVP: _____

At this party just as the one mentioned above, you can serve any type of dinner that you choose—from a hamburger cookout to Mexican fiesta. Decorate according to your menu choice or use clocks as centerpieces and decorations.

Couples games
You may want to include one of the following activities after dinner and opening gifts.

Nearly-Wed Game. Ask the groom to leave the room. The guests will create four or five questions to be answered by the bride. The questions should have something to do with the couple, their dating relationship, or their future plans. Be sure to write down the questions and the bride's answers. Bring the groom back into the room and ask him the same questions. He is to try to match what he thinks his bride may have answered. For each right answer, the groom will receive a flower to give to his bride.

Next, send the bride out of the room and allow the guests to ask four or five questions of the groom. Don't forget to write down the questions and answers. For each correct answer, the bride receives a golf tee or ball or other sports paraphernalia to give to her groom.

Interesting Interviews. Before the party, interview the bride and groom separately, asking them to tell the story of how they met and how he proposed. Tape-record their responses (be sure to tell them that you are recording their answers) and play the interviews at the party. It will be fun to hear each version and catch the similarities and differences.

Cohostess Etiquette

When more than one person gives the shower there are several areas to consider. The person who is having the shower at her home should do less of the food preparation, since she is preparing the house. Perhaps drinks and one easy-to-prepare food item are enough for the house provider. Other responsibilities to divide include invitations, addressing and mailing, receiving reservations, and purchasing the gift for the bride or couple.

Each participant should take on several responsibilities. Food preparation should be divided as equally as possible. Remind everyone to keep the receipts. After the party is over, take all receipts, total them, and divide the amount by the number of hostesses. Each hostess will then subtract the amount that she spent. The answer will tell her how much she owes to the hostess general pool. If she comes up with a negative amount (which means she spent more than the average), then she should receive the amount of difference from the pool.

Do this accounting work after the shower is over and everyone else has left. There is nothing more embarrassing to the honoree and guests of a shower than to find all of the hostesses huddled in the kitchen tallying the shower cost. Believe me, I've seen it, and it's not a pretty sight!

The most important thing is for the hostesses to communicate often and keep informed of the number of RSVPs and the general organization and schedule of the shower. You may want to appoint an organizational leader to ensure good communication. It helps to have one person who is considering all of the details for the group and making sure everything is accomplished.

Final Note

Marriage is one of the most significant decisions made in a lifetime. What a joy to be a part of the celebration process! In the Bible we learn that God uses the beauty and commitment of marriage as a picture of Christ and the church. Ephesians 5:25–26 says, "And you husbands, show the same kind of love to your wives as Christ showed to the Church when he died for her, to make her holy and clean" (TLB).

We are told in the Bible that there will be an incredible wedding one day in heaven between Christ and His Bride. It is described in Revelation 19:7 as The Marriage Supper of the Lamb. The invitation to this wedding is available to all who will accept it. Don't miss the most important wedding of all!

> Believe on the Lord Jesus Christ and you will be saved.
>
> Acts 16:31

Chapter 12

SHOWERS OF NEWBORN BLESSINGS

SHOWER SCHEDULE • 1.5–2 HOURS

There is no need to be strict about the schedule of the party, but you may want to generally follow this schedule of events:

20 Minutes: Greetings and punch
40 Minutes: Eating
30–60 Minutes: Activities and opening presents

She's going to have a baby! What an exciting time in the life of a young family. A baby shower is the perfect way to honor the expecting mother and welcome the precious newborn baby. Whether you choose to have the shower before the baby comes or have a "Sip and See" once the baby has arrived, you're sure to bring joy to the growing family.

Baby Shower Invitations

The best time for baby showers is Saturdays (morning, noon, or afternoon). Check with the mother-to-be to see what time is best for her and if there are others who would like to join you in hostessing the event. Perhaps you know of other close friends of the honoree that may want to help in giving the shower. Please read the notes on shower Cohostess Etiquette at the end of the previous chapter to assist you in your planning.

As you decide to provide a shower for your special friend, consider the expecting mother's needs. If this is her first child, she could use a miscellaneous shower. If this is not the first child, the mother could possibly use more help in the area of consumables, such as diapers, wipes, liquids, lotions, and casseroles. Recently I heard of a shower (given for a mother having her fifth child) in which the guests were each asked to bring a children's book. Each guest purchased one of their family favorites and signed it inside with a special blessing to the new baby. What a delightful idea!

There are a variety of creative routes you can take with the shower invitations depending on budget and number of people invited. Keep in mind that most anything can be sent through the mail. I have received a baby bottle as a shower invitation with the party information on the inside. I have also received a folded and taped diaper with the party information on the inside. Perhaps you want to attach the information to a baby rattle using a pink and blue ribbon and mail it in a postage tube.

A simple invitation can be made using pastel colored 5 x 7 cards. Print the invitation information in the center of the card and attach a baby diaper pin using hot glue. No matter which creative invitation you choose, your general wording can be as follows:

It's a Baby Shower!
Let's celebrate
the coming of the newest member
of the (family's name) Family.
Join us for (lunch, brunch, or tea)

Date:_____

Time: _____

Address: _____

RSVP: _____

Add additional information as to the type of shower or gender of the baby. If you are planning a "Sip and See" and the mother would prefer that guests do not bring gifts, you can add, "(mother's name) would like to invite you to see precious (baby's name), but requests no gifts please."

For a shower that I recently cohosted (several weeks after the baby was born), we added the following statement at the mother's request. "If you have already brought a gift to (mother and baby's names), please join us for the party, but no further gifts please."

Baby Shower Decorations

For the decorations I suggest you choose one theme and decorate throughout the party areas with this idea. A likely source for the theme may come from the baby's nursery decor. Ask the mother-to-be if she has a theme for her nursery. Possibilities include teddy bears, Precious Moments, Noah's ark, rainbow colors, rocking horses. If you know the baby's gender then you may want to base the color scheme accordingly. Decorate with the theme in mind using posters, pictures, figurines, and toys. For example, if you choose teddy bears, place teddy bears throughout the party area tying colorful bows around their necks. Use the bears for centerpieces and coffee table decorations. They can also hold flowers or balloons. Depending on your budget, you may even find miniature ones to use as place card holders, favors, or prizes.

Add color-coordinated balloons to your decor both indoors and at the front door. Tie baby rattles, teething rings, or pacifiers to the ends of the balloons. Purchase a floral corsage for the mother-to-be or make a usable corsage by wiring together two rattles, along with a pair of baby socks, pins, and other needed items.

Arrival Activities

One hostess should be assigned to the door to greet the guests and help them with name tags. Name tags are helpful at showers.

You may find printed baby shower name tags or keep with your theme and use cutouts or stickers to decorate your name tags. Ask the guests to write their names and their association with the honoree. It is helpful to have the honored mother (if she is physically able) to stand close by the door to welcome and introduce the guests to one another.

Another hostess should be in charge of offering coffee, tea, or punch to the guests who have just arrived. Here is a good punch recipe that will work for brunches, luncheons, or teas.

Precious Punch

2 quarts chilled cranberry juice cocktail
7 cups chilled orange-flavored carbonated drink
1 quart raspberry sherbet

❖ Combine cranberry juice and orange drink in a large punch bowl. Add scoops of sherbet to the mixture and serve immediately.
❖ Yields: 18 punch cup servings.

Baby Shower Menu

Frozen Fruit
Spinach Quiche
Party Sausage Pinwheels
Baby-Block Mini-Cakes

Frozen Fruit

1 cup fruit cocktail or fruit cut into pieces
½ cup seedless grapes   ½ cup watermelon balls
1 (32 oz) bottle ginger ale, chilled
mint leaves

❖ Combine fruits; place into an 8 x 8 metal pan. Pour ginger ale over fruit and freeze 1½–2 hours or until mixture is a mush. Serve in fancy plastic cups or glasses; garnish with mint leaves.
❖ Yields 8 servings.

Spinach Quiche

2 (9 inch) frozen pie crusts, partially baked
8 oz Gruyère cheese, grated
2 cups heavy cream or milk
½ cup flour   6 eggs
1 medium onion, minced   1½ tsp salt
½ tsp pepper
1 (10 oz) pkg frozen spinach; let thaw and dry with towel

❖ Sprinkle grated cheese onto pie crusts. Beat cream with flour, add eggs, onion, seasonings, and beat well. Add spinach and blend. Pour into pie crusts. Bake in 400° preheated oven for 40 minutes, or until a knife inserted near the center comes out clean.
❖ Yields 16 servings.

Party Sausage Pinwheels

2 cups biscuit mix   1 lb ground pork sausage
  chopped chives

❖ Prepare biscuit mix according to package directions. Roll dough out on a lightly floured surface into a rectangle that measures about 15 x 18 and about ⅛ inch thick.
❖ Dot entire surface with pieces of fresh pork sausage; sprinkle with chives. Cut dough in half crosswise and roll each half, jelly roll fashion, toward the center, making 2 rolls. Chill for easy slicing. You can also freeze the rolls.
❖ Cut each roll into ½-inch slices. Arrange ½ inch apart in a shallow, ungreased baking dish. Bake at 450° for 15 minutes or until golden brown. Drain on absorbent paper. Serve hot.
❖ Yields about 4 dozen.

Baby Block Mini-Cakes

1 box white cake mix

❖ Prepare cake mix according to instructions. Pour into a 9 x 13 greased and floured pan. Bake according to instructions and cool. Carefully remove the cake from the pan.
❖ Trim cake to achieve straight sides and level top in order to create square cubes. Cut cake lengthwise into 4 equal strips, then cut each strip into 6 equal pieces.

Icing:

6	cups powdered sugar	½	cup water
⅓	cup light corn syrup	¼	cup margarine, melted
1	tsp vanilla		

❖ Combine all ingredients, stir until powdered sugar is blended, then beat at high speed until smooth. Add 2 or 3 tsp. of water if necessary until icing is of the consistency to drizzle over cake blocks. Spoon icing evenly over the tops and sides of blocks. Allow icing to set. Using colored frosting, decorating bags, tips, and candies, decorate cake blocks to resemble baby blocks.

❖ Yields 24 cake blocks.

After most of the guests have arrived, encourage them to get a plate of food. Decide with your cohostesses before the party whether you are going to serve buffet-style or offer prepared plates. Generally baby showers are not an "eat at the table" event unless you have a small guest list or lots of table space.

Menu Additions

For a brunch, add your favorite muffins or coffee cake to the menu. If this is a luncheon, add a green salad with dressing, tomatoes, and croutons. For a tea, serve quiche in thin slices, or finger sandwiches. Consider adding scones, cream, and jelly.

Baby Shower Activities

Games and activities are not a necessary part of a shower, but most people enjoy a few short activities that add fun interaction to the party. Pick and choose activities that suit your particular group.

Blessings

Give each guest a pen and a card (possibly cut out in theme shape or printed with a baby border). Ask the shower guests to write a blessing to the baby. Example: May God bless (baby's name if you know it) with an obedient spirit. Collect the cards and place them in a photo album along with pictures of the shower, as a gift to the mother. Variation: You may want to ask your guests to write a prayer which they will commit to pray for the baby sometime during that day, or month or year. Example: I will pray that the baby grows to have a loving spirit and a heart for God.

Guesswork

If the baby has not yet arrived on the scene, have your guests try and guess the birth date, sex, length, weight, hair, and eye color of the baby. Ask the shower guests to write down their guesses on an index card. You may want to read them out loud or make a chart for everyone to see the guesses. Assure the guests that the winner (the person who has the greatest amount correct) will be informed after the baby arrives.

What's My Food?

Purchase eight different jars of baby food and replace the labels with stickers numbering one to eight. Place the jars on a tray decorated with ribbons. Give each participant a pencil and paper. The object of the game is to guess the type of food that is in each jar. Each guest will write her answers one through eight and then the hostess will tell the correct answers. The players who get the highest number of correct answers, win a prize. Prizes may be a small recipe book, recipe cards, or cookies.

Baby Concentration

Before the party, fill a basket or diaper bag with several small baby items, such as socks, teethers, brush and comb, pacifiers, nail clippers, washcloths, travel size lotions and powders. (Share the expenses with a cohostess.) Pass the basket or diaper bag to each guest so that they can see all of its contents. Do this rather quickly. Provide paper and pens for the guests to write as many baby items as they can remember. The one who remembers the most wins a small prize, such as a candle, potpourri, or candy. The mother-to-be wins no matter what—she gets to keep all of the baby items.

Opening Presents
As the honoree opens her gifts, assign one hostess to write down the gifts and the givers, and another hostess to collect the wrapping paper and assist in passing the gifts. Ask the mother-to-be to tell the group how she knows the person whose gift she is opening. Display the gifts on a nearby table. When the honoree finishes, allow her to thank the guests and tell of any plans she has as far as nursery, hospital, and visiting options.

Final Note

Children are a gift from God and baby showers are a gift that we can give to our expectant friends. Allow God to use your hospitality in a special way by giving showers and opening your home to others. As I think about the blessing of having children, I am reminded of the even greater blessing of being one of God's children.

> How great is the love the Father has lavished on us, that we should be called children of God! And that is what we are!
>
> 1 JOHN 3:1, NIV

Chapter 13

FAREWELL FIESTA

FIESTA SCHEDULE • 1.5–2 HOURS	
20 Minutes:	Arrival, hors D'oeuvres, mingle
40 Minutes:	Dinner
30-60 Minutes:	Dessert, farewell activities

Adios! Au revoir! Arrivederci! Ciao! Good-byes are never easy when someone moves away. Make this Farewell Fiesta a memorable occasion using the creative activities provided in this chapter. Invitations, dinner recipes, and group gift ideas are all included. This fiesta theme works for any type of party, whether it's a send-off for a favorite family or just a friendly fellowship!

Invitations

You must first decide if you want to make this Farewell Fiesta a surprise party or not. If it is a surprise, make sure that everyone is invited that should be invited. Even if the party is not a surprise, you can surprise the family that is leaving with a special and memorable gift mentioned later in this chapter.

Evenings, preferably weekend evenings, are the best time for this gathering. If the moving family has children, you will need to decide if children will be included in the party and clearly state that on the invitation.

The invitations can be written on brightly colored card-stock with a miniature tissue paper flower attached on the front. Flowers can easily be made by cutting several 2 x 3-inch rectangles of tissue paper. Stack five sheets one on top of the other, gather in the center and secure with floral wire. Fluff each sheet of tissue paper individually, and a paper flower will form. Tape or glue the small flower to the front side of the invitation. The information will read as follows:

It's a Farewell Fiesta
to say adios to our amigos

The (last name of family) Family

Time: _____

Date: _____

Address: _____

RSVP: _____

Group Gifts

Information about group gifts will need to be included in the invitation. Several weeks before the party, begin putting together a meaningful gift from the guests. Choose one of the following ideas, or perhaps you have an idea of your own. Be sure to include your expectations in the invitation and send the invitations out about two and a half weeks in advance so the guests have time to do their part.

Memories Book

Ask guests to write a note or poem about what the honorees mean to them. Encourage them to include memories of special times spent together and thoughts on what they appreciate about their friendship. A photograph that can be contributed to the book would be helpful.

You may want to include a blank piece of stationery or bordered paper with the invitation so that each guest's entry looks consistent. Add Polaroid pictures from the Farewell Fiesta to the Memories Book as well.

Video Memories
Create a video of each guest telling their fond memories and sentiments of the leaving family. In your invitation you will need to include a note asking your guests to prepare a small message to be videotaped when they arrive at the party.

At the party, assign a cohost to take the guests into another room and videotape their message. Encourage everyone to be themselves. If they want to be funny, let them show their true colors. You may want to start or end the video using pictures of the honored family in a variety of settings. Add background music as you tape the photos. A perfect song for the occasion is Michael W. Smith's "Friends." Show the video at the end of the evening and then give it to the honored family.

Friendship Quilt
Send each guest a 6 x 6 cross-stitch fabric square (14 point) along with their invitation. Include a note telling them to decorate their square using paints, cross-stitch, appliqués, buttons, or whatever craft they can do themselves. Each guest's square should in some way represent their own family and should include their name. Ask the guests to return the squares at least one and a half weeks before the party. Invitations with this project in mind should go out three weeks before the party to give the guests enough time to complete their square. You will need to select material for a backing to the quilt, and purchase quilt batting for inside. If you are not a seamstress, ask someone to help you put the quilt squares together, or hire a seamstress to do the job.

Friendship Frame and Photo
Purchase a plastic 8 x 10 frame along with a light-colored matte to surround the picture. As guests arrive, ask them to sign their names on the matting. Take several group photos at the party in order to select the best one. When the photos are developed

after the party, choose the best one to have enlarged to 8 x 10 size. Present the pictureless frame the night of the party telling them that the picture will be coming in the next few days.

It may be nice to have reprints made to send to your guests as a memory of the special evening. If you would like to have the project finished on the night of the party, use a Polaroid camera to take individual pictures of the guests. Put them together in a collage and place in a large plastic frame, using the signed matte as a border.

Signed Craft
There are a variety of crafts that can be painted or made with all of the guests' names on them. Ideas include a large bird house, a ceramic bowl or large plate, a wall hanging (fabric banner), or even a vase holding silk flowers.

Festive Decorations
Use a variety of bright-colored crepe papers to decorate throughout the house. Purchase several piñatas for the event. If you have trouble locating piñatas, use colorful balloons instead. Lay Mexican blankets on the tables over the tablecloths. Napkins, plates, and cups should be in a variety of bright colors. Make large paper flower arrangements to serve as centerpieces and decorations. Check with a local travel agency for posters of Mexico. Don't forget to play Mexican music during the party.

Make a large poster or banner for the door or inside the house with the words: *Vaya Con Dios* (Go with God). Allow all the guests to sign their names to the poster using colorful markers.

Arrival
Provide chips, salsa, bean dip, queso, guacamole dip. Serve chips in the rim of Mexican sombrero hats. You will need two cohosts: one to replenish chips, dips, and drinks; the other to organize the gifts as the guests arrive. Depending on which gift you have chosen, your cohost may need to take videos,

gather pictures to put in the albums, etc. Offer bright-colored name tags for the guests.

Fruity Mexican Punch

2 lemons	4 limes
2 oranges, sliced and halved	2 quarts grape juice
2½ cups lemon-lime soda	

❖ Cut lemons and limes into wedges. In large pitcher, combine fruit pieces and grape juice, slightly squeezing fruit pieces. Chill for several hours. Pour into punch bowl and add soda just before serving.
❖ Yields 12 punch cup servings.

Mexican Buffet Menu

South of the Border Salad
Make-Your-Own-Taco Bar
Mama's Sour Cream Chicken Enchiladas
Marguerite's Mexican Rice
Zacatecas Beans
Cinnamon Pecan Squares
Sopaipillas

South of the Border Salad

1 (16 oz) pkg frozen whole kernel corn, cooked, drained, and cooled	
3 Tbsp Italian salad dressing	
1 Tbsp cider vinegar	¼ tsp dry mustard
⅛ tsp celery salt	⅛ tsp white pepper
½ cup sliced mushrooms	
⅓ cup unpeeled, chopped cucumber	
3 Tbsp thinly sliced green onions	
3 Tbsp chopped green pepper	
3 Tbsp chopped red pepper	

❖ Combine salad dressing, vinegar, mustard, salt, and pepper and mix well. Add corn and remaining ingredients; toss gently. Cover and chill 3–hours.
❖ Yields 6–8 servings.

Make-Your-Own-Taco Bar
A taco bar is a delicious and practical addition to any Mexican buffet, especially if children are involved. Taco bars provide the opportunity to make your own just the way you like it. Provide grated cheese, taco meat (ground beef with taco seasonings), sliced seasoned chicken, chopped or grated lettuce, diced tomatoes, chopped onions, hard taco shells, and soft tortillas.

Mama's Sour Cream Chicken Enchiladas

1 small chicken (cooked, boned, and chopped)
1½ cups grated cheddar or longhorn cheese
1 doz flour tortillas   1 medium onion, chopped
1 can cream of chicken soup
1 cup grated Monterey Jack cheese
1 can chopped green chilies 1 cup sour cream

❖ Mix chopped chicken, onion, and cheese together. Steam tortillas to soften them. Put chicken mixture in tortillas (1–2 Tbsp per tortilla, and roll tightly). Place in a greased 9 x 13 baking dish.
❖ Combine cream of chicken soup, green chilies, and sour cream. Pour over enchiladas and bake at 350° for 30 minutes. Sprinkle Monterey Jack cheese on top and bake again until cheese melts.
❖ Yields 8–10 servings

Marguerite's Mexican Rice

1 cup white rice   1 Tbsp oil
2 cups water   ⅛ tsp salt
½ cup salsa   ½ cup frozen corn, thawed
½ cup carrots, chopped into small pieces
½ cup frozen peas, thawed

❖ Fry rice in 1 Tbsp of oil in a large skillet until browned. Add water, salsa, salt, and vegetables to skillet and cook for 20–25 minutes until all liquid is absorbed.
❖ Yields 8–10 servings.

Zacatecas Beans

16 oz pkg of red beans	⅛ tsp salt
¼ cup chopped cilantro	1 tomato, diced
½ cup chopped onion	3 slices of bacon, chopped

❖ Cook beans according to package directions adding salt.
❖ Add remaining ingredients and simmer for 10 minutes.
❖ Yields 10 servings.

Choose one of the following desserts. The Cinnamon Pecan Squares require less preparation and can be made several days ahead of time.

Cinnamon Pecan Squares

1 cup butter or margarine	1 cup sugar
1 egg, separated	1 tsp vanilla extract
¼ tsp ground nutmeg	1 tsp ground cinnamon
2 cups all-purpose flour	¾ tsp baking powder
1¼ cups chopped pecans	

❖ Preheat oven to 350°. In a medium bowl, beat together butter or margarine, sugar, egg yolk, vanilla, nutmeg, and cinnamon until well blended. Gradually beat in flour and baking powder until thoroughly blended. Press mixture evenly in an ungreased 15 x 10 jellyroll pan. Beat egg white slightly with a fork. Brush over top of dough. Sprinkle evenly with pecans, lightly pressing into dough to secure. Bake 25–30 minute or until golden. Cool 10 minutes in pan; then cut cookies into squares. Cool completely in pan.
❖ Yields about 25–35 cookies.

Sopaipillas

4 cups all-purpose flour (sifted)	
1¼ tsp salt	3 tsp baking powder
⅓ cup sugar	2 Tbsp shortening
milk (about ¾ cup)	4 beaten eggs

❖ Mix flour with other dry ingredients, rub in shortening with finger tips, and add milk and eggs to make a soft dough just firm enough to roll. Allow dough to stand for 30–60 minutes, then on lightly flowered board roll ¼ inch thick and cut in diamond-shaped pieces. Fry in deep fat at

about 400°. Turn at once so they will puff evenly, then turn
back to brown both sides. Drain on paper towels. Serve
with honey and cinnamon sugar.
❖ Yields 4 dozen.

After-Dinner Fun and Fellowship

Sharing
Let the couple who is moving share a little about their plans.
You may choose to do this in an interview fashion, asking the
couple about their new house, job plans, new church, etc.
Next, ask some of the guests to share about special times they
have experienced as friends together. If you have chosen to do
the Video Memories, play it at this time.

Create an Acrostic
Using colorful heavy paper, write (calligraphy is nice) the
honored family's name down the side of the paper. Ask the
group to share ideas that would create an acrostic describing
their feelings about the family. Place the finished product in a
large plastic frame and give the acrostic as a keepsake for the
family.

Artistic Outlet
This activity works best with a light-hearted group. Divide the
guests into smaller groups consisting of four or five people.
Each group is then to create an original poem or rap song
about the family that is leaving.

Example:

> *The Smiths are leaving and we are most sad,*
> *But we like to reflect on the times we had.*
> *There are many memories that make us glad,*
> *So sit back and listen for just a tad . . . .*

Be sure to tape-record or videotape the productions and per-
formances.

Group Photo
Gather everyone together for a variety of group photographs. Take several types of photos. One with everyone smiling, one with everyone showing a sad expression, one crazy photo, and one ham-it-up photo. Put these pictures in a gift photo album for the family that is leaving.

Send Them Off with a Prayer
As the party comes to a close, have a time of prayer for the family that is leaving. Depending on the group, you may want to have one person lead the prayer, or you can open it up to anyone who wants to pray. It would be nice to hand everyone a list containing the family's prayer requests and new address. Contact the honorees before the party to learn of specific needs they want to share with the group.

Final Note

Do not limit yourself to only the Mexican theme. A Western or Hawaiian party would work just as well for a going-away party (see chaps. 7 and 8 of this book). You may choose to simply do a cookout with no theme at all. Whatever you decide you can still apply all the games and activities in this chapter. I encourage you to set a personal goal of corresponding to your friends after they have moved. The first year that the family is gone you may want to write more frequently, knowing that it takes a while to feel adjusted and make new friends. As time goes on, commit to writing twice a year, once on your friend's birthday and once on Jesus' birthday.

> I thank my God upon every remembrance of you, always in every prayer of mine making request for you all with joy.
>
> PHILIPPIANS 1:3:4

*Special thanks to Margaritta Oneida for her helpful input for this chapter.

Chapter 14

TOP OF THE WORLD BIRTHDAY CELEBRATION

CELEBRATION SCHEDULE • 1.5 HOURS	
30 Minutes:	*Guest arrival, mingle, special preparations*
60 Minutes:	*Surprise! (if it is one), eat, and tribute*
30 Minutes:	*Birthday cake, open presents or cards*

No "Over the Hill" pouting at this party! Age milestones do not need to be doom and gloom occasions, but rather celebrations of a good life and hopefully many wonderful years ahead. Plan a surprise party or a scheduled event using the fantastic ideas found in this chapter to honor your loved one on his or her special day.

Global Invitations

Since the theme of the party is "On Top of the World," you will want to include a picture or stickers of the world on your invitation. At craft stores you can find world stickers or perhaps a bordered paper with a world or international flags.

You may want to make your own world invitation by cutting a circle out of blue poster board and applying green construction paper as the land. You could even add a photo of the birthday person sitting on top of the world. (Simply find a photo of the honored guest in a sitting position. Make copies using the negatives or photocopy. Cut out the picture and glue it to the globe.) Your information should read as follows:

Person's name

is on top of the world
as he (she) turns **XX !!!**

Come celebrate this magnificent milestone on

Date: _____

Time: _____

Address: _____

RSVP: _____

Gifts or No Gifts

It is important to politely mention the gift situation on the invitation. A pleasant way to state that you would rather the guests not bring gifts is to say, "Cards only please," or "No presents, just your presence." If you have invited a group of close friends, you may want them to bring a gag gift. Be sure to mention this in the invitation, yet you do not want anyone to feel obligated to bring a gift. It helps to say, "Gag gifts only," or "Gag gifts if you like," or "Tasteful gag gifts only."

To Surprise or Not to Surprise

This party is best as a surprise party, because most people are not willing to agree to a planned celebration centered around themselves. The surprise element allows for the much-deserved party without letting the honoree in on the event. Be sure to state on the invitation that it is a surprise event and be careful about the phone number that you give to RSVP. Guests should arrive thirty minutes before the honoree.

Go to extra lengths to find all of the special friends that the birthday person would want to have present at the party. Check address books, ask friends and relatives if they know others who should be included. You do not want to make the mistake of leaving out someone who is close or special to the birthday person.

When should you not surprise someone? When the honoree is a person who does not like surprises. Yes, there are genuinely people who dislike surprises, and they abhor the thought of someone throwing them a surprise party. If your friend or spouse has mentioned to you in the past that he or she does not like being surprised, then *believe it!* Remember whom you are honoring. If the birthday person will not be pleased or amused, then you are wasting your time. For the non-surprise person, just schedule a simple, planned birthday dinner with several close friends. You can still use the birthday ideas in this chapter, and everyone will be truly happy.

A BRIEF WARNING: Please do not plan a surprise party for someone at their own home, unless you are planning to clean the home yourself before the party. Case in point: Cathy's husband decided at the last minute to have a surprise party for her after church one Sunday. He quickly invited several couples over for ice cream and cake. (I don't know about you, but when I leave to go to church on Sunday, my house is far from immaculate.) My friend was horrified when she arrived home and found all of her friends at her own home with the clutter of the weekend scattered about. Needless to say, this was not a blissful moment nor a happy birthday. So please be considerate and thoughtful when it comes to the location of the event. Consider having the party at alternative locations, such as a friend's house, a favorite restaurant, the local civic center, or a country club.

Creative Ways to Surprise

There are several fun ways to get the surprisee to the intended location. Try one of the following or concoct your own plan.

Scavenger Hunt. Hand deliver (or fax) a clue to the birthday person to lead them on a scavenger hunt ending at the party location.

Friendly Dinner Invitation. Have a close friend or old buddy call to invite the birthday person to dinner. The friend will pick the birthday celebrity up and take him to the party location. The guests will all be at the restaurant ready to yell, "Surprise!"

After-Dinner Scenario. Take the birthday person out to dinner with the plan to go to the movies. Leave something at home that you need to get before the movies (such as glasses, more money, movie coupon), saying that you need to stop home for just a minute to get it. When you arrive at home, "Surprise!"

Reverse Surprise. Tell the guests to gather down the street from the birthday person's house. Make sure that the birthday person will be at home. Then at a given time the party guests will ring the doorbell and yell, "Surprise!" from the front porch. Take the birthday person out to eat or bring food inside. Please note the warning I gave earlier concerning surprising the birthday person at home.

International Decorations!

In keeping with the "Top of the World" theme, decorate with international flags and globes. You can even find inexpensive inflatable globes to hang from the ceiling. Your color scheme can be green and blue napkins, plates, and tablecloths. Add balloons and streamers along with posters displaying pictures of the honoree from childhood to the present.

Guest Arrival Activities

While you are waiting for the guest of honor to arrive, keep your guests entertained by offering them snacks and something to drink. Provide a blank book, giant card, or T-shirt for everyone to sign as they arrive. Hand out buttons, hats, or T-shirts that say "(birthday person's name) is (age)!" or "(name) is on top of the world at (age) !" or "I saw (name) turn (age) !"

You can also play a "True or False" game as you wait. Gather little-known (nonembarrassing) facts about the birthday person's life and write them on slips of paper. Write some false statements as well and put them all in a basket together. Guests take turns drawing slips of paper and guessing if it is true or false.

Birthday Menu
Dinner Salad with Vinaigrette Dressing
Beef and Spinach Lasagna
Garlic Bread or Dinner Rolls
Vanilla Wafer Coconut Cake

You may choose to serve an entire dinner or just cake and ice cream. Specify on the invitation so that your guests know what to expect. The above menu will work well for either a sit-down dinner or buffet for a larger group. If you are serving a smaller, more intimate group, you may want to consider the menu for a "Formal Dinner with Class" (chap. 10).

Dinner Salad with Vinaigrette Dressing

    1 cup thinly sliced celery
1½ cups shredded green or red cabbage
    3 Tbsp thinly sliced green onions
   ¾ cup sliced carrots
   ¾ cup thinly sliced radishes
4–5 cups romaine or other crisp lettuce

❖ Tear lettuce into bite-size pieces. Combine all vegetables in a large bowl.

Dressing
   ⅓ cup sugar   ½ tsp seasoned salt,
   ½ tsp minced garlic   3 Tbsp cider or wine vinegar

❖ In a jar with a tight-fitting lid, combine dressing ingredients; shake well. Pour dressing over salad, toss well, and serve immediately.
❖ Yields about 8 servings.

Beef and Spinach Lasagna

Assemble this delicious dish up to a day ahead of time, refrigerate until ready to bake.

1 medium onion, chopped   1 clove garlic, minced
2 Tbsp olive or salad oil   1 lb ground beef
1 (3 or 4 oz) can sliced mushrooms
1 (8 oz) can tomato sauce   1 (6 oz) can tomato paste
2 tsp salt   1 tsp dried oregano
¾ cup water   1 egg
1 (10 oz) pkg frozen chopped spinach, thawed, drained
⅓ cup grated Parmesan cheese 1 cup cream-style cottage cheese
1 (8 oz) pkg lasagna, cooked and drained
1 (8 oz) pkg Mozzarella cheese slices, cut in strips

❖ In a medium-sized frying pan, lightly brown onion and garlic in 1 Tbsp of the oil; add ground beef, cook until brown.
  Drain off excess grease. Blend in mushrooms (including
  mushroom liquid), tomato sauce, tomato paste, 1 tsp of the
  salt, oregano, and water; simmer 15 minutes.
❖ Meanwhile, mix egg with the spinach, cottage cheese,
  Parmesan cheese, remaining 1 Tbsp oil, and 1 tsp salt. Pour
  half the meat sauce in a 9 x 13 baking pan and cover with
  a layer of half the lasagna. Spread all the spinach mixture
  over lasagna. Complete layers with remaining lasagna and
  meat sauce. Cover and bake at 350° for 45 minutes.
  Remove cover and arrange strips of cheese on top; bake for
  15 minutes longer. Serve hot.
❖ Yields 10 servings.

Serve garlic bread or your favorite dinner rolls with the lasagna
and salad.

Vanilla Wafer Coconut Cake

½ lb butter   2 cups sugar
6 eggs   ½ cup milk
1 (12 oz) box of vanilla wafers, crushed
1 (7 oz) pkg flaked coconut 1 cup finely chopped pecans

❖ Cream together butter and sugar. Add eggs one at a time,
  beating until thick and fluffy. Add vanilla wafers and milk,
  alternately. Fold in coconut and pecans. Turn the batter into
  a greased and floured 9 x 13 baking pan. Bake at 275° for
  1 hour and 15 minutes. Cake will be moist but firm. Cool
  10 minutes in pan and then invert and cool on cake rack.
  Ice with vanilla or lemon icing when cool. Sprinkle
  coconut flakes on top if desired.
❖ Yields 12-15 servings.

After-Dinner Fun and Fellowship

Ways to Honor the Birthday Person

Once the surprise has taken place, you will want to pay tribute to the honoree in a special way. Choose one or a combination of the ideas below to show honor and appreciation to the birthday celebrity.

This Is Your Life. Several weeks before the party, contact friends and relatives of the birthday person who live out of town or who haven't seen the honoree in a while. Ask these people to come up with a funny or memorable story about the birthday person. Before the party, tape-record the friend or family member telling the story, over the phone if necessary. Bring in as many of these mystery speakers as possible to be present at the event.

On the night of the event, you will need to keep the mystery guests hidden when everyone else yells "surprise." Quickly move into the "This Is Your Life" event before eating. Play the audio tape and see if the birthday person can identify the speaker. If the mystery guest is present, he should come out at this time. As a memento of the evening, put together a scrapbook with photographs and letters from guests and mystery guests. Write on the cover, THIS IS YOUR LIFE.

Accentuate The Positive. Choose one of the outstanding qualities about the birthday person and take it to the extreme, honoring him or her for that area of interest. For instance, if the honoree loves horses and enjoys horsemanship, then decorate the party area with equestrian paraphernalia. Present the horselover with a laurel of roses when she arrives. Give each guest a stick horse to hold for the surprise. Other ideas include each of the guests dressing up in athletic outfits for a sports fanatic, dressing up with glasses and holding books for the book lover, or dressing like fashion models for the perfect vogue dresser. Inform your guests over the phone concerning this particular theme, so that you can plan and formulate ideas together.

Memories Presentation. Gather photographs of the birthday person from childhood to the present. You will need to contact family and various friends to get a good compilation of photos. Make a video or slide presentation using the photos and adding background music. If you have negatives, you can take them to a photo center and have them made into slides. There are some studios that will put your photographs and music together in video form for easy presentation. Check your local directory for listings of services of this type.

Appreciation Talk. What better gift can you give to a person than to tell him about the qualities you most appreciate in him. Whether this is a sit-down dinner or a buffet, once everyone has been served, take time to go around the room and have each guest tell of a character quality they appreciate in the honoree. This is a meaningful and important time. Be sure to video or audio tape the comments.

Gag Gifts. If gag gifts were brought to the event, allow individual guests to present their gifts while everyone is enjoying birthday cake.

Group Gifts. Group gifts and activities suggested in chapter 13 (Farewell Fiesta) are easily adaptable to this birthday celebration as well.

If possible, videotape the events of the evening and present the video as a special gift to the honoree.

Final Note

Birthdays are a special time to honor one another. As you prepare this party event, remember this is an opportunity to say to the birthday celebrity that you are thankful that God has brought him or her into your life. Think of this celebration as a gift you are giving to the honoree. It is important to keep the right perspective, as it creates a much more joyful and relaxed atmosphere for both hostess and guests.

> Love each other with brotherly affection and take delight in honoring each other.
>
> ROMANS 12:10, TLB

Chapter 15

HATS OFF TO YOU!
CONGRATULATIONS
PARTY

SCHEDULE • 2 HOURS	
30 Minutes:	Arrival, Group Banner or Hats
45 Minutes:	Surprise, dinner, and interview
45 Minutes:	Dessert and activities

Congratulations! What an accomplishment, and now it's time to celebrate! Invite friends and family to wear their favorite hat to a party that honors the completion of a great endeavor. It could be a job promotion, an athletic triumph, a personal goal, or graduation. Whatever the occasion, it is a privilege to "rejoice with those who rejoice" (Rom. 12:15)!

Top Hat Invitations

When you consider throwing a party to congratulate a friend or family member, you will need to decide if it is going to be a surprise party or not. As I mentioned in the previous chapter, a surprise party may be appropriate for an event such as this since most people are not willing to agree to a party planned in their honor.

The most important aspect to consider for a surprise party is if the honored guest likes to be surprised or if he detests it.

Do not throw a surprise party for someone who dislikes being surprised. He will not appreciate the planning and hard work that goes into the event. Know your honoree. You can always celebrate with a few friends at a preplanned dinner party.

In considering whom to invite, keep in mind that this is a celebration to show appreciation for what the honoree has done. Those invited should be loved ones who are truly excited and want to share their congratulations. Please do not invite distant friends or acquaintances to fill the room with people. This party can be just as special (if not more) with a small group as it can be with a large crowd.

Your invitations will be in the form of a top hat. You can use black poster board cut in the shape of a top hat or use a white poster and glue black satin fabric on the front to look like the surface of a hat. If you are artistically challenged (as I am), ask an artistic friend to draw a stencil for you to copy.

You can also create your invitations on computer. It may be hard to find bordered paper with hats on it, but you are likely to find paper that has something to do with the guest of honor's accomplishment (sports, writing, flying, etc.). Use stickers from craft stores to enhance your invitation. The information can read as follows:

Hats off to
<u>Guest of Honor</u>
For **<u>accomplishment</u>**
Join us for a Congratulations Celebration!

Date:_____

Time: _____

Address: _____

RSVP: _____

Please wear your favorite hat to the party!!!

Include in the invitation information whether the event is a surprise and if dinner is included or if it is simply a dessert party.

Honorary Decorations

Decorate according to the accomplishment being celebrated. If there are pictures, trophies, or medals, then display them along with other related items. Display pictures of your celebrity guest from childhood to the present, if it won't embarrass him or her. Use the honoree's favorite colors to decorate with balloons and party supplies. Don't forget background music—perhaps the honoree's favorite tunes or theme music from *Chariots of Fire* or *Rocky.*

Arrival Activities

If this is a surprise party, the guests should arrive thirty minutes before the guest of honor. Name tags are important, and make every effort to introduce the guests to one another. You will need several fun activities to interest your guests during the waiting time. Here are several intriguing ideas.

Group Banner
Purchase butcher or mural paper to make a large banner or create one from a computer. The banner could say "**Hats off to Guest's Name** " Or perhaps, "**We're Proud of You!**" Or, "**Congratulations!**" Add photographs of the honoree.

Each guest should then sign the banner with a few sentences of congratulatory sentiments. Use a variety of colored markers. Take a picture of the group holding the completed banner. Buy a photo album as a gift for the guest of honor and place the picture of the group in the front of the album. You may want to grid off the banner into sections so that after the party you can cut the banner into pieces and put the individual messages into the album.

Make Your Own Hat
Instead of asking your guests to wear their favorite hats, you may want to consider allowing your guests to make their own hats when they arrive. Provide materials for your guests to

"go wild" creating the hat of their dreams. Award prizes for originality, tallest, widest, most colorful, etc. Use a variety of materials such as foil, newspaper, strips of poster board, tissue paper, foam material, netting, and other fabrics. Be sure that you have a good supply of glue, tape, and staples.

Take pictures of each of the guests wearing their hats and put them in a photo album. Ask guests to write special notes of congratulations that can also be placed in the photo album.

Surprise!
You will find strategies on how to pull off the element of surprise in the previous chapter. When the guest of honor arrives, everyone will yell "Surprise" and then take off their hats and say in unison, "Hats off to you!"

Celebration Menu
Colorful Fruit Medley
Chicken Divan
Buttered Corn
Dinner Rolls

Chocolate Toffee Delight
After the guest of honor has had time to recover from the surprise and to greet everyone, invite the guests to get a plate of food and sit down. This will work well as a buffet, but if you have a small group you may prefer a sit-down dinner.

Colorful Fruit Medley

1 can sliced peaches, drained   2 bananas, sliced
1 red apple, cored, sliced, and cut into bite-size pieces
1 (20 oz) can of pineapple chunks, with juice
¾ cup raisins   ¾ cup chopped walnuts
  Add raspberries or chopped strawberries if in season.

❖ Combine all ingredients including pineapple juice. Serve in small cups or on a large lettuce leaf.
❖ Yields approximately 8–10 servings.

Chicken Divan

2 (10 oz) pkgs frozen broccoli cuts, cooked, drained
1 2½–3 lb chicken, cooked, boned, sliced
2 (10 oz) cans cream of chicken soup
1 cup mayonnaise   1 Tbsp lemon juice
½ tsp curry powder   1 (10 oz) pkg grated cheddar cheese

❖ Place broccoli in bottom of 9 x 13 greased baking dish. Put chicken on top of broccoli. Heat soup then add mayonnaise, lemon juice, and curry powder. Stir to blend and pour over chicken and broccoli. Cover with grated cheese, bake 25 minutes at 325°, until hot and bubbly.

❖ Yields 8–10 servings.

Chicken Divan can be served with the above salad, buttered corn, and dinner rolls.

Conversation Booster

Ask your guests to share the answer to the following question with those sitting around them during dinner. "If you could achieve one great accomplishment in life, what would it be?"

After-Dinner Fun and Fellowship

Interview with the Honored Guest

As your guests finish their meal, direct their attention to the honoree. Prepare a special chair for the celebrity to sit in during his important interview. Remember to allow the honoree to get his food first so that he can be finished eating in time for the interview.

Make a microphone using foil wrapped around a small tube or use a microphone that belongs to other equipment (perhaps from a children's toy or an old tape recorder). You may want to take on the persona of a famous talk show host or interviewer. Ask the guest of honor several important questions pertaining to his or her accomplishment. Use the following questions to get you started.

• When did you decide to begin this incredible endeavor?

- What was the most difficult obstacle in your pursuit of this accomplishment?
- What did you find most fulfilling?
- Now that you have achieved such great heights, what do you plan to do next?

After you have finished with your questions, open the floor to questions from the audience. When a guest has a question for the honoree, have him stand up while you bring the microphone to him. It would be helpful to have guests think of questions before the interview.

Make little comments in between the questions, as do talk show hosts. Ham it up! The humor will be delightful! Make captions on small poster boards similar to those you see on talk shows. Tell of the honoree's accomplishment stating the same information in different ways. Here is an example for a person who ran a marathon:

- "Ran marathon at age 22."
- "Boy from Kansas runs first marathon."
- "Hometown Hero ran 26.2 miles."

Ask a cohost or assistant to flash the signs now and then under the honoree's face. Take pictures or videos of this entertaining event.

Delightful Dessert

After the interview, invite everyone to enjoy dessert and coffee. During this time you may choose to mingle and talk or you can play the "Game of Greatness." You will need to discern if your combination of guests are the type of people that would enjoy playing a game together.

Chocolate Toffee Delight

2 cups whipping cream	1 (5 ½ oz) can chocolate syrup
½ tsp vanilla	1 angel food cake
1 lb toffee candy, crushed	

❖ Whip cream until it starts to thicken; gradually pour in chocolate syrup and vanilla, and beat until thick. Cut angel food cake in half crosswise forming two layers. (It is easier to cut the cake if you place it in the freezer several hours before cutting.) Spread some of the whipped chocolate cream in the center and sprinkle half of the crushed toffee candy over the cream. Place the top layer on the cake and frost top and sides of cake with the rest of the chocolate cream. Sprinkle with remaining toffee. Refrigerate at least 2 hours before serving.

❖ Yields 10 servings.

Game of Greatness

Ask everyone to think of someone famous whom they admire. It could be someone from history or the present day. Hand each guest an index card and ask them to write down one fact about their hero. Gather all of the cards and one by one read the facts. All guests will attempt to guess who is being described, while the person who wrote the fact remains silent until it is time to reveal the answer. You can play this game in teams as well.

Example: Despite her physical challenges, this woman wrote more than two thousand great works used by many Christians today.

Answer: Fanny Crosby, hymn writer

Final Note

Although we may accomplish great things on this earth, we must always remember that if we want to be great in God's kingdom, we must learn to have a servant's heart. After the disciples James and John arrogantly, or ignorantly, asked to sit at Jesus right and left sides in glory, Jesus taught these words about greatness in the kingdom of God:

Whoever desires to become great among you shall be your servant.

MARK 10:43

HOLIDAY PARTIES

O magnify the LORD with me, and let us exalt His name together.

PSALM 34:3

New Year's Eve Countdown Celebration

As the host or hostess, you will need to determine the length of the party that suits you. I suggest three to four hours. Keep the schedule loose, playing games, mingling, and munching. The last hour of the party should be reserved for the "make your own sundaes," midnight countdown, and discussion.

Ring in the New Year with friends and family! A bountiful buffet of food and a plentiful supply of activities will provide hours of entertainment for your guests. Midnight sundaes, a creative countdown, and a prayer for the coming year top off this wonderful night of celebration.

Party Hat Invitations

How many people do you want to invite to your New Year's Eve party? Consider whether you will be more comfortable entertaining a house full of people or simply enjoying a meaningful time with a few close friends. Talk it over with possible cohosts and discuss the purpose for the party. The party activities and food described in this chapter can be adapted to your party preference.

Purchase inexpensive, cone-shaped party hats. You can find New Year's hats at a local party supply store. Type the information you see below on bright-colored paper and glue it to the front of the hat. Send in a 5 x 7 envelope and include a party blower along with the invitation.

LET'S CELEBRATE
THE NEW YEAR TOGETHER!

Party Time: _____ December 31
Join us for food, fun, and fellowship!
Come and go or stay the whole evening
to welcome in the new year together.
Your RSVP is important: _____
_____ attire.

Note: As you plan the party, decide if you want it to be a semi-formal event or a casual gathering and specify clearly on the invitation.

The timing for this event is your personal preference as well. Some may choose to have the party from 9:00 P.M. to 1:00 A.M. While others are more comfortable with an earlier event from 7:00 P.M. to 11:00 P.M. (You can ring in the New Year with an earlier time zone!)

Festive Decorations

Black, white, and metallics (silver and gold) are perfect colors for this event. Decorate black poster boards with glitter lettering to make a welcome sign. Using the same idea, you can make other "Happy New Year!" signs to hang in various places. Purchase dozens of black and white helium balloons with metallic ribbons to decorate the main rooms of the party. Do not tie the balloons to objects, just let them hang from the ceiling for special effect.

You will probably have Christmas lights still in place, which will add to the party decorations outside of your home.

Purchase white Christmas lights at the after-Christmas sales and surround your welcome sign with lights. Use white Christmas lights inside as well, outlining doors and around the food table, and accenting any signs.

Cover the food table with a black tablecloth and spread metallic confetti around the table. Transform a flower arrangement into a New Year's centerpiece by simply adding party blowers and curled ribbon. Play the past year's popular Christian music hits on the stereo. Add to the aroma of the event by simmering potpourri in various places around the house.

Games and Activities

As guests arrive give them a name tag (decorate with glitter sequins or confetti if you like). The atmosphere of the party begins at the door with your "excited-to-see-you" greeting. Ask a cohost or friend to be your food assistant, offering drinks and replenishing food as you greet at the door. Start the party off with an ice breaker game or move right into the variety of games listed below.

When considering the games, pick and choose. You do not need to play all of the games suggested in this chapter. Discern the personality of your group. Are they game players? Would they rather mingle with a smattering of trivia questions? Are they the type that would enjoy group games throughout the evening? Or are they more of the "make-yourself-at-home," eat-a-little, do-a-puzzle type of crowd? You know your guests. Plan accordingly. Allow for balance between the flow of the evening and planned activities. Most importantly, smile and have fun with your guests!

Fascinating Facts from the Year Past

Usually newspapers or magazines will have articles of the "Year in Review" in their late December issues. Use these articles as a resource for creating trivia questions. Choose your method of playing the trivia game. You can have one particular time when you play the game with everyone in a group. My favorite way to play is to ring a bell now and then throughout the evening, getting everyone's attention and then asking a trivia question. Present small prizes to the winners of each question.

Party Puzzles

Provide several two-hundred-piece puzzles that guests can work on during the party. If you want to make puzzles the main event of the party, you could hand each guest a piece from a puzzle as he or she arrives. This would designate the puzzle on which the guest would work throughout the evening. (You may want to number the puzzle pieces to help the guest find the right puzzle.) Award prizes for the first puzzle finished.

Table Games

Provide a variety of games, such as Life, Monopoly, Parcheesi, Clue, Scrabble, and Uno for your guests. Set the games up at different tables and let everyone choose the game that they want to play, or designate the game that the guests will play by letting them randomly choose a game piece out of a bag.

Famous Labels

Before the party make a list of famous people of the past year. These can be media or entertainment personalities, politicians, sports figures, scientists, artists, musicians, or anyone of notoriety. Make copies of the list to give to each guest. Beside each name on the list, players are to write two descriptive words of the person using the initials of that person's name. Encourage players to use only positive descriptions. After players have completed their list, read the answers and vote on the best descriptions. You can let guests play in teams or as couples.

If your guests are fairly close friends with each other, you may want to make a list of guest's names and ask the players to write descriptions using the initials. Here is an example:

Carrie Smith—Caring Sympathetic
Bill Goodwin—Brave Godfearing
Terry Kelly—Talented Kindhearted

Costume Party in a Box

Did you want to have a costume party but were afraid to ask? Well, your dream has come true! Instruct your guests to create their own costumes at the party. This activity can be done individually, as couples, or in teams. Provide players with a box containing a variety of supplies, such as newspaper, crepe paper, poster, foam material, felt, feathers, tape and scissors. In an allotted period of time (e.g., 10 minutes), let each player or group of players go to it! If you are playing as couples or teams, then each player on the team should be costumed according to a group theme.

You will be amazed and pleased at the incredible creations. Play upbeat music and allow each team to model their creations. Videotape and photograph the guests in costume. Send the pictures to your guests after the party as a memory of their fashion statements.

Quiz Show

Divide the players into teams consisting of four or five players each (use birthday months to help divide). Give each team a flag, flashlight, bell, or something for them to signify that they want to answer. Award five points to the first team that gives the correct answer. You can make the game more interesting by adding bonus point questions or taking away points for wrong answers. Use questions from your favorite trivia game or make up your own questions using the dictionary, world almanac, or use the "Quotable Quotes" game in chapter 10.

Salad Bar Game

Believe it or not, food can make an interesting New Years activity. This salad bar game idea was submitted to me by Melinda Seibert, who says this game has become an annual event with her family and friends. The hostess prepares a typical salad bar: lettuce, tomatoes, carrots, celery, croutons, grated cheese, olives, and more if you like. The object of this game is to create a salad that portrays something significant about the past year. Each player must explain their creation.

Sound *corny*? *Lettuce* encourage you to try. It is amazing what you can do with the ingredients for a salad. Imagine a church made out of croutons and ranch dressing. Or can you picture a mother and child made out of tomatoes and olives? Once the salads are made and explained, then everyone votes on their favorite. Prizes can be anything that has to do with salad. Melinda's group has traditionally given a kitchen magnet that looks like a vegetable.

Several years ago Melinda won the contest when she made a plain lettuce and dressing salad. She explained that in the previous year she had learned that self-worth is not based on performance but on who we are in Christ. Isn't it amazing what we can share from a salad?!

Along with your salad bar, you will want to have other munchies as well. I suggest a menu of soup, salad, and sandwiches with a variety of chips, dips, and popcorn for snacking throughout the night.

Countdown Menu

New Year's Eve Crab Dip
Frosty the Cheese Ball
Grand Ole Deli Sandwich
New Year's Eve Hot Mug of Soup
Ice Cream Sundae Bar

New Year's Eve Crab Dip

1 (8 oz) pkg cream cheese, softened
1 (6½ oz) can crab claw meat, drained
1 tsp mayonnaise   paprika
   parsley sprigs

❖ Blend cream cheese, crabmeat, and mayonnaise. Sprinkle with paprika and chill before serving. Garnish with parsley sprigs.

Frosty the Cheese Ball

2 (8 oz) packages cream cheese, softened
2 cups crumbled Roquefort cheese
2 Tbsp grated onion   1½ tsp prepared mustard
1 Tbsp Worcestershire sauce
⅛ tsp cayenne pepper

❖ Combine cheeses, onion, mustard, Worcestershire sauce, and cayenne pepper; mix until smooth. Cover and chill for 30 minutes or until firm enough to shape. Shape into 3 balls using 1½ cups for first, 1 cup for second, and ½ cup for third. Arrange one on top of another to form a snowman. Use food items such as raisins, cherries, and a small cut of carrot for the face and buttons. Make or purchase a doll-size hat for the top.
❖ This cheese ball could also be shaped into one ball and rolled in chopped pecans.

Grand Ole Deli Sandwich

1 French bread loaf, sliced through the center, horizontally
¼ cup margarine, softened   ½ cup dairy sour cream
2 tsp prepared mustard   ¼ tsp garlic powder
  dash dried dill weed   variety of deli meats and cheeses

❖ Add sour cream, mustard, garlic powder, and dill weed to butter and beat together until smooth. Spread mixture on both slices of bread and layer meats and cheeses so that a variety are distributed throughout the sandwich. Place the top slice on the sandwich and cut every 1½–2 inches.
❖ Yields approximately 8–10 servings.

New Year's Eve Hot Mug of Soup

1 (46 oz) can V-8 juice   2 (10½ oz) cans beef broth
5 Tbsp lemon juice   5 Tbsp Worcestershire sauce
1½ tsp salt   ½ tsp Tabasco

❖ Combine all ingredients in large pot heating over medium heat or prepare in crock pot. Serve in mugs.
❖ Yields 12 servings.

Gift idea: Personalize each mug and give as souvenir of the party.

Ice Cream Sundae Bar
At about 11:15 begin setting out the ingredients for the ice cream sundaes. You will want to provide several flavors of ice cream and a variety of toppings. Popular toppings include hot fudge (great recipe found in chap. 6 of this book), chocolate syrup, butterscotch syrup, pineapple sauce, strawberry topping, coconut, chocolate chips, and caramel. You do not need to purchase all of these, but do provide a good variety and remember the whipped cream, nuts, and cherries!

One or two people should be in charge of dishing out scoops of ice cream while guests create their own sundae with toppings deluxe. If possible, serve the sundaes in plastic parfait glasses. Provide a variety of simple cookies to eat with the ice cream. At the sundae bar set out blowers, noise makers, and party hats so that everyone will be ready for the countdown.

Creative Countdown

Here's a new and unique way to count down the final ten seconds before midnight. Earlier in the evening divide your guests into ten small groups, giving each group a small, neon-colored poster board and markers. Feel free to add more craft supplies if your budget allows. Assign each group a number, one through ten. The object is to display the number in a creative way on the poster somehow incorporating each group member's New Year's resolution.

You will see some wild and wacky ways to portray numbers. As the midnight hour approaches, ask each group to stand together in numerical order. It adds to the anticipation if each group keeps their poster a carefully guarded secret until the actual countdown. Ten seconds before midnight each subgroup will hold their poster up for all to see as the whole group counts in descending order from ten to one. After the midnight celebration, hang the posters around the room and let group members explain them.

Prayer

After all is settled and the new year has been welcomed, it is very meaningful to join with your guests to pray for the coming year, asking God's continued blessings.

Encourage your friends to choose a "yearly verse" from the Bible. This verse should be one on which they will focus and memorize during the year. Possible verses could be Hebrews 12:1–2: "Therefore we also, since we are surrounded by so great a cloud of witnesses, let us lay aside every weight, and the sin which so easily ensnares us, and let us run with endurance the race that is set before us, looking unto Jesus, the author and finisher of our faith, who for the joy that was set before Him endured the cross, despising the shame, and has sat down at the right hand of the throne of God." Or Galatians 2:20: "I have been crucified with Christ; it is no longer I who live, but Christ lives in me; and the life which I now live in the flesh I live by faith in the Son of God, who loved me and gave Himself for me."

Allow some people to share their verses with the rest of the group. Provide nice paper and decorate an inexpensive plastic frame with confetti or festive stickers to display the verse.

Party Prizes and Favors

Certainly there is no need, requirement, or expectation to give favors at the end of the party, but if you feel so inclined, here are a few suggestions. These ideas are also helpful for game prizes mentioned earlier.

- Small calendars or day planners
- Colorful pens or pencils
- Box of chocolates
- Key chains
- Scripture memory cards
- Decorated frames
- Hand-painted mugs or cups

- Visors or hats with the new year on them
- Flowers, real or artificial
- Small bags of flavored coffee

Put in black gift bags with white tissue paper or metallic shredded paper. Write guests' names with paint pens on the bags.

Final Note

The new year represents a time of new beginnings. This is a perfect time for all of us to ask the Lord to show us areas of our lives that need refining. I'm so glad the Christian walk is one of becoming a new person. Let's allow God to continue to mold and make us into useful vessels for Him.

> But now, O LORD, You are our Father; We are the clay, and You our potter; And we all are the work of Your hand.
>
> ISAIAH 64:8

Chapter 17

HEARTS OF LOVE VALENTINE'S DINNER

SCHEDULE • 1.5–2 HOURS	
20 Minutes:	Greetings, Hearts Game
30–40 Minutes:	Dinner and conversation
40 Minutes:	Dessert and games

LOVERS LIMIT • 6–10 PEOPLE

Love is in the air with this heart-filled dinner party, perfect for married couples and singles alike. Invite your guests to enjoy a delicious Cornish Game Hen dinner and Heart Tart dessert. Delightful games and activities are added to make this a lovely evening to remember.

Lovely Invitations

Using red poster board, cut large hearts for each guest or guest couple. Write the party information with a white paint pen in cursive handwriting. Attach small candy hearts to the invitation and include a few more candies in the envelope. Your information will read as follows:

> *Roses are red;*
> *Violets are blue.*
> *We've (or I've) planned a special dinner*
> *Just for you!*

The place is _____;

_____ is the date.

We'll start at _____,
So please don't be late!
RSVP: _____.

Decorations from the Heart

Red and white hearts will be your major theme and should be carried throughout the party rooms. Use red and white poster board, foam board, or felt fabric to make as many hearts as you possibly can to hang on the front door and inside walls. Add paper lace doilies as well. Red and white helium balloons dangling from the ceiling make a lovely addition. Chocolate heart candies wrapped in red foil can be distributed on coffee tables and around the main food table.

Cover your dinner tables with red tablecloths, placing lace cloths on top. Lay a long-stemmed rose at each female's place setting with a small name card tied to the rose. Place a carnation boutonniere with a name card at each male's place setting. Crystal candle holders or a candelabra holding red or white candles create a lovely decoration at the center of the table. Use small glass bowls to float flower buds near the base of the candles. Since this is a formal dinner, you will want to use your china dinnerware at the table. For cloth napkins, use the fan-folded napkin idea explained in chapter 1.

Candy bowls and dishes filled with heart candies (the ones with little two-word sentiments stamped on them) or red hots should be placed around the party room. Play soft romantic music. Use floral potpourri and candles for scent. Dim the lights allowing the candlelight to illuminate the party.

Arrival Activities

Greet each guest at the door with a warm smile and hug, allowing a cohost or hired help to take care of preparations in the kitchen. Offer name tags and punch as guests arrive. Use regular white name tags and decorate with heart stickers around the edges.

The following punch recipe makes a splendid welcome:

Valentine's Punch

1 cup boiling water
1 (3 oz) pkg raspberry flavored gelatin
1 (6 oz) can frozen lemonade   3   cups cold water
1 (32 oz) bottle cranberry juice cocktail, chilled
1 (28 oz) bottle grapefruit carbonated beverage, chilled

❖ Pour boiling water over the gelatin; stir to dissolve. Stir in lemonade concentrate. Pour into large punch bowl. Stir cold water and cranberry juice cocktail. Slowly pour in grapefruit beverage; stir gently to mix. Add ice or an ice ring.
❖ Yields 12–15 servings.

In addition to the punch, you may want to have some simple hors d'oeuvres available. Nuts, cheese and cracker plates, and vegetable trays are excellent ideas for finger foods to have available while the guests play the "Hearts Game" and mingle.

Hearts Game

Cut out red and white hearts about four inches in diameter. Write one Biblical Lovers Trivia question (found below) on each heart. Next, make one jagged cut across the heart to separate it into two pieces. Make the cut a little different for each heart. Put all of the pieces in a decorated basket.

Ask your guests to choose one heart half when they arrive. Their objective will be to search and find the person who has the other half. Once they put it together they are to try and answer the trivia question. When they think they know the answer, they must check with you. Award a prize to each couple who comes to you with a correct answer. You may choose to use these questions as an after-dinner trivia game instead of as an icebreaker.

Biblical Lovers Trivia Questions

Q: Who paid a great price for his wife and then was deceived?
A: Jacob (and Rachel)

Q: What couple met while she worked in his wheat field?
A: Boaz and Ruth

Q: What couple lied to God and paid a heavy price?
A: Ananias and Sapphira

Q: This man married his half sister.
A: Abraham (and Sarah)

Q: What couple had their first-born son die as a result of their sin?
A: David and Bathsheba

Q: This husband had the perfect adopted son.
A: Joseph (and Mary)

Q: Which couple played favorites with their twin boys?
A: Isaac and Rebekah

Q: This couple shared in Paul's ministry.
A: Priscilla and Aquilla

Q: What husband was speechless while waiting for his first son to be born?
A: Zechariah (and Elizabeth)

Q: This couple was involved in a detrimental hair cut.
A: Samson and Delilah

Prizes for this game could be simple items bearing hearts, such as note pads or pens or give small boxes of chocolate hearts.

Romantic Menu

Sweetheart Salad
Cornish Hen with Rice Stuffing
Peas and Mushrooms in Dill Sauce
Heart Biscuits
Red Fruit Heart Tarts
Chocolate Dessert Truffles

This party is best suited for a sit-down dinner. The above menu will help you plan the event. Arrange Cornish hen, peas, several half slices of orange and sprigs of parsley on each plate for a colorful and inviting presentation.

Sweetheart Salad

    1 (8 oz) pkg cream cheese, softened
    1 cup sugar   3 bananas, sliced
 8-12 ounces whipped topping
    1 (10 oz) pkg frozen strawberries, partially thawed

❖ Mix together cream cheese and sugar until well blended. Fold in whipped topping, strawberries, and bananas. Spoon into 9 x 13 serving dish. Freeze overnight. Using large heart cookie cutter as a guide, cut heart shapes and serve on a lettuce leaf.

❖ Yields 8-12 servings.

Cornish Hen with Rice Stuffing

 4-6 (1-1½ lb) Cornish game hens
   ½ cup finely chopped onion ⅔ cup uncooked regular rice
    4 Tbsp butter or margarine, melted
    2 Tbsp lemon juice   1 can cream of celery soup
   ⅓ cup finely chopped celery 1 Tbsp chives
    1 Tbsp parsley flakes   1½ cups water
    2 chicken bouillon cubes   salt, pepper, melted butter

❖ After cleaning out game hen, sprinkle cavity with salt and pepper. Saute onion, celery, and rice in butter for five minutes or until rice is golden. Add lemon juice, soup, chives, parsley, water, and bouillon cubes; bring to a boil. Cover, reduce to medium heat, and cook for 25 minutes.

❖ Spoon mixture loosely into cavities. Place hens breast side up in a shallow baking dish and cover with foil. Bake at 375° for 30 minutes. Uncover and bake 1½ hours more. During the last 30 minutes, baste with butter.

❖ Yields 4-6.

Peas and Mushrooms in Dill Sauce

    1 (16 oz) pkg frozen sweet peas
    1 cup sliced fresh mushrooms
   ½ cup sour cream   ¼ tsp dill weed

⅛ tsp salt   1 cup water
     pepper

❖ Bring peas and mushrooms to boil in 1 cup water. Cover and cook over medium high heat about 3 minutes or until vegetables are tender; drain. Stir in sour cream, dill, salt, and a dash of pepper.
❖ Yields 4–6 servings.

Heart Biscuits

Add heart-shaped biscuits to the menu. Prepare biscuit mix adding red food coloring to make the dough. Use a heart-shaped, heavily floured cookie cutter to cut the biscuit dough before baking. Brush with melted butter mixed with several drops of red food coloring.

Conversation Booster

Place little slips of paper containing conversational questions in a heart-shaped box. As everyone enjoys dinner, pass around the box and let each person pull a question. Use the following questions or make up your own.

- What does the term *true love* mean to you?
- Explain "love at first sight."
- In your opinion, what is the greatest love story you have ever heard?
- What kind of music do you consider to be romantic?
- Why do you think the heart is used as a symbol for love?
- What does it mean to love someone with all of your heart?
- What is one aspect that you love about Valentines Day?
- Which do you prefer as a sentiment of love: candy, flowers, or a note?
- When you want to express love to another person, what do you do; send a note, give a gift, or do something nice for them?
- Where would you choose to go for a romantic dinner for two?

Dessert

Serve the following dessert delights with delicious coffee.

Red Fruit Heart Tarts

1 9-inch pie crust, unbaked, room temperature
1 tsp flour   3 Tbsp red currant jelly
1 (8 oz) pkg cream cheese, softened
¼ cup powdered sugar   ¼ cup orange juice
¾ cup strawberries or raspberries, halved

❖ Sprinkle room temperature pie crust with flour and smooth out any folds or wrinkles. Turn crust flour-side down onto an ungreased cookie sheet. Cut crust into individual heart shapes. (Use a large heart-shaped cookie cutter or a cardboard heart as a guide.) Fold edges in ½ inch and flute. Prick crust with fork several times. Bake in preheated 450° oven for 9–11 minutes or until golden brown.

❖ In a small saucepan, melt jelly with one tsp of orange juice. Brush a thin layer over tart crusts. Combine cream cheese, powdered sugar, and 1 Tbsp of orange juice, beating until smooth. Spread over crust. Arrange fruit halves, cut-side down on the cream cheese mixture. Brush with remaining jelly mixture. Refrigerate until serving time.

❖ Serve tarts on a dessert plate garnished with mint leaves and the delicious truffles detailed below.

❖ Yields 8—10 servings.

Chocolate Dessert Truffles

4 oz semisweet chocolate pieces, coarsely chopped
2 Tbsp whipping cream
2 Tbsp ground sweet chocolate or cocoa

❖ Place semisweet chocolate and cream in a 1–1½ quart pan over lowest possible heat. Stir constantly until chocolate is melted and well blended with cream. Cover and chill just until chocolate cream mixture is firm enough to hold its shape (about 40 minutes). While waiting, spread ground chocolate on a small plate or on a piece of waxed paper. Using your fingers or 2 spoons, quickly shape about 1 tsp of the chocolate cream at a time into a ball; then roll in the ground chocolate until completely coated. Arrange truffles in a single layer in a shallow container. Cover and refrigerate until firm to serve, or store up to 2 weeks.

❖ Yields about 12 truffles.

After-Dinner Fun and Fellowship

After dinner, invite your guests to join you in the living room for some interesting trivia and enjoyable games. Choose activities from the following list that fit your group's personality.

Story of Saint Valentine

Read or tell the story of Saint Valentine so that your guests may have a greater appreciation of the holiday and of one of God's servants.

> The story of Saint Valentine begins in the third century. It concerns an oppressive Roman emperor (Claudius II) and a humble Christian martyr (Valentinus).
>
> Claudius had made a decree that all Romans were to worship twelve gods, and the penalty of disobedience was death. He even went as far as to say that those who associated with Christians should die. Valentinus was dedicated to Christ and His service and bravely continued practicing his beliefs. Soon he was arrested and imprisoned.
>
> A remarkable event occurred in the last weeks of Valentinus' life. Recognizing that Valentinus was a man of learning, the jailer asked if he might bring his daughter to be tutored by the prisoner. The jailer's daughter, Julia, had been blind since birth.
>
> Julia was a lovely young girl with a quick mind. Valentinus taught her about Rome's rich history and about the world of nature. He taught her arithmetic and most importantly taught her about God. Julia came to learn much about the world through the dedicated teaching of Valentinus.
>
> One day she asked Valentinus if God really heard the prayers of His people. Of course Valentinus answered that He does. Julia then admitted that every morning and every night she would pray asking God to allow her to see.

Valentinus answered, "God does what is best for us if we will only believe in Him."

Julia affirmed that she did believe, and she knelt and grasped Valentinus' hands. They prayed together that God would heal her from blindness so that she could see His wonderful creation.

Suddenly there was a brilliant light in the prison cell. Julia cried, "I can see, I can see!"

Valentinus exclaimed, "Praise be to God!"

On the night before he died, Valentinus wrote a brief note to Julia. The note told Julia to stay close to God and was signed, "From Your Valentine."

Valentinus was put to death the next day, February 14, A.D. 270. Tradition has it that Julia planted a pink-blossomed almond tree near his grave. Today, the almond tree remains a symbol of abiding love and friendship. Messages of affection, love, and devotion are exchanged around the world on this special day in remembrance of a devoted saint and his kindness toward others.

Most Romantic Story Contest

If your party consists of married couples, allow each couple to tell the story of how they met and how the spouse proposed. After everyone has shared their story, vote on the most romantic story and award a box of chocolates to the winning couple.

Famous Couples

Divide into two groups. A quick way to divide into teams is to put two colors of candies (e.g., pink and red) into a small white sack. Each person picks out one candy with the color determining the team. You can also allow couples to play as teams.

The host or hostess will declare a category (found below) and each team must write down the names of famous couples that fit into the category within a one-minute time period. The team with the greatest number of legitimate names wins ten points for their team. Play several rounds. Here are some probable categories.

- Famous couples in current sitcoms.
- Famous newscast couples.
- Famous couples in politics.
- Famous couples of black-and-white television.
- Famous fairy tale couples.
- Famous couples of rerun sitcoms.
- Famous couples of movies, past and present.
- Famous couples from classical literature.

Hide God's Word in Your Heart

If you feel it is appropriate with your group of guests, you may want to include this activity at the close of the party. In Deuteronomy 6:5 the Israelites were told to love God with all of their heart, soul, and strength. Discuss with your guests what it means to love God in this way. Encourage your guests to commit this verse to memory and hide it in their hearts. You may want to give each guest a small heart-shaped box and include a card or paper with this verse printed on it.

Final Note

Love, love, love! Isn't Valentine's Day wonderful? But what could be more wonderful than God's love for us? This Valentine's Day, reflect on the greatest love of all—God's perfect love for His people.

> For as high as the heavens are above the earth, so great is His lovingkindness toward those who fear Him. As far as the east is from the west, so far has He removed our transgressions from us. Just as a father has compassion on his children, so the LORD has compassion on those who fear Him.
>
> PSALM 103:11–13, NASB

Chapter 18

HE IS RISEN!
EASTER CELEBRATION

SCHEDULE • 2 HOURS
40 Minutes: Greetings, children's activities
40 Minutes: Resurrection story, prayer, dinner
20 Minutes: After-dinner activities

"Christ is risen!" "Christ is risen indeed!" Easter is a celebration of hope for all Christians. Enjoy a meaningful time with friends and family as you gather to eat a savory Easter meal and play "eggciting" games, reflecting on our resurrected Lord.

Easter Invitations

With this particular gathering, you may want to extend the invitation to your guests over the phone. Generally this event includes family members and close friends, yet you should always be open to others that the Lord may lead you to invite. Remember, this is one of the greatest celebrations we have as Christians, and the focus should not be on the perfect buffet, but on honoring the risen Savior together as believers.

If you would like to use invitations, here is a creative idea. Send an artificial Easter lily with a note attached that reads:

CHRIST IS RISEN INDEED!
Let's celebrate together on
Easter Sunday

1:00 P.M

address

Dinner and activities for both
adults and children
are part of this jubilant event.

Another invitation idea is an empty tomb, made from brown poster board, cut in the shape of Christ's burial cave. Cut a white piece of paper to glue onto the poster board as the opening to the tomb. Write the invitation information inside. Attach another piece of brown poster board to represent the stone that was rolled in front of the tomb. If kids are receiving the invitation, it is fun to make a movable stone roll in front of the opening, simply by attaching the paper stone with a brass brad.

Jubilee Decorations

Decorations for this event focus on the risen Savior and the new life we have in Him. There is no greater hope and victory than that of the message of Easter. Christ died for our sins and rose from the grave so that we may have victory over sin and death.

An open Bible and cross placed on a table near the entrance serve as reminders of Christ's resurrection. "Stained-glass" windows make lovely decorations. Using black poster board, cut a rectangle shape with an arch on the top. Cut out the inside of the window so that the poster board makes a frame. Use pieces of colored tissue paper or cellophane taped together to create the stained-glass-effect. Make your own or allow the children to make the stained glass windows as an arrival activity. Display the finished products on windows throughout the house. Colorful eggs may also be used as part of the decorating theme because they provide a wonderful example of the Trinity (see Eggsallent Eggsample later in this chapter).

Use flowers galore! Easter lilies and baskets of fresh flowers should adorn your main rooms. Tulips, daisies, sunflowers, and pansies are all wonderful spring decorative flowers. Take a little extra time to plant spring flowers outside your front entrance as well. For your door, consider a lovely floral wreath or a Styrofoam cross covered with ribbon and decorated with flowers.

Your dinner table can be decorated with a pastel or lace tablecloth, china, and coordinating napkins. As place cards, use small tufts of plastic Easter grass and one colored, hard-boiled egg. Write each guest's name on the egg at their place setting. You may want to consider a small table just to the side of the adult table for the children. Decorate the children's table using a pastel paper tablecloth, plates, and cups.

Grassy baskets filled with colored eggs can be scattered about the room much to the delight of younger ones. Candy dishes filled with pastel-colored wrapped or coated candies make a lovely decoration as well, but watch the little ones who may see the dishes as an opportunity to overload on chocolate!

Don't forget the potpourri scents and background music. At Christian bookstores you can find instrumental praise music or favorite hymns that can provide a pleasant and gentle sound.

Greetings and Children's Activities

Greet your guests with joyfulness as you welcome them to this special celebration. Give each person a warm hug and then say, "Christ is risen!" Those who know the traditional response will say, "Christ is risen indeed!" If your arriving guests do not know the response, tell them about this special way of greeting Christians on Easter, then practice again.

If you have young ones at this Easter gathering, you may want to consider the following activities. Keep in mind that a good arrival activity for children is to have them make a stained-glass window as described in the decorations section above.

Easter Mural (5–8-year-olds)
An Easter mural makes a good arrival activity, or it can be made after dinner. You will need mural paper or large butcher paper

and a variety of crayons or washable markers for the kids. Find a wide-open space with a hard surface to lay the mural down. If it is nice weather, you could use the back porch area.

In a small basket, place pieces of paper with the name of an object or part of the Easter story written on each: cross, empty tomb, angel, soldiers, women coming to the tomb, sun. When your young guests arrive, ask them to pick a paper out of the basket. Show the children the mural and ask them to draw or color the part that is on their slip of paper.

For younger children (3–4-year-olds), you may want to outline the entire picture in black marker so that they can easily color the picture without having to draw it themselves. Even the two-year-olds can help by simply coloring the sky or the grass. When the mural is complete, display it for all to see. Let each child tell about the part they drew for the mural.

Eggsallent Eggsample (5–10-year-olds)

Gather the children together to show them some fascinating concepts about the egg. Before the party prepare some hard boiled eggs and color them if you like. Use one hard-boiled egg to share about the Trinity—God three in one. You may say something like this:

> The reason we like to think about eggs and new life on Easter is that we are celebrating Jesus' coming back to life after dying on the cross. Because Jesus rose from the dead, we, too, have the hope of eternal life after we die. The Bible also says that when we trust in Christ, we have a new life in Him and that the old life is passed away. This egg reminds me of the new life that I have in Christ.
>
> The egg also reminds me of the Trinity, God three in one. Let me show you. The hard outer shell makes me think of God the Father, our rock and our refuge (Ps. 18:2). Just as this hard shell protects the egg, so God is our shield and protector (Ps. 28:7).

As we look at the inside of the egg [break open the egg], we find the egg white. The pure and perfect white reminds me of the pure and perfect lamb of God who gave His life for me (Ex. 12:5; 1 Pet. 1:19). Because of Jesus' sacrifice, my sin has become white as snow (Isa. 1:18).

The third part of the egg is the yolk. The yolk is the nourishing part of the egg, just as the Holy Spirit nourishes us. He is our helper (John 14:16) and comforter (Acts 9:31). He helps us understand right from wrong (John 16:8–11). The yolk is in the center of the egg reminding us that the Holy Spirit comes to reside in us when we become a Christian (Rom. 8:11).

Just as all three parts make up an entire egg, so God in three parts makes up the Trinity. I wonder if He gave us an egg as an "eggsample" of Himself and the new life that we have when we trust in Him.

Egg Hunt (Children of all ages)

Provide a small basket for each child at the event. You can purchase baskets (if budget allows) or use one of these special options to make baskets out of materials that you have around the house:

Coffee Cans. Before the party, paint cans in pastel colors with rope handles attached. Fill with plastic grass or shredded paper.

Grocery Sacks. Cut several inches off the top of the grocery sack, leaving a small hump in the center for the handle. Cut a hole to complete the handle. Let the children decorate their own baskets with crayons and stickers.

Paper Plate Baskets. Staple a poster board handle to two sides of a paper plate, allowing the plate to curve and form a basket. You may want to leave the basket as is or curve the other two sides to close in the basket.

Once you have your baskets prepared, then you are ready

for a very special egg hunt. A wonderful idea for older kids (6 and up) is to fill the small plastic eggs with items that have something to do with the Easter story: a piece of wood, a purple cloth, a thorn, a nail, a stone, pieces of silver, white bandage material, small angel, etc. Leave one egg empty to remind the children of the empty tomb. FamilyLife Ministries has a product called Resurrection Eggs that uses this same idea. (To order a carton [one dozen filled eggs], contact FamilyLife, 3900 North Rodney Parham, Little Rock, Arkansas, 72212, (501) 223-8663.)

After the hunt, gather everyone together for the opening of the eggs. Talk about the different items. You may want to have other eggs with candy and coins available as small gifts to the children.

Communion (believers only)

If your adult guests are all believers, you may want to consider taking communion together before dinner. You will need crackers or unleavened bread and small cups of grape juice. First Corinthians 11:23–26 is a good reference to use as you practice this remembrance of Christ's death for us.

This would be a good opportunity for children to learn about Passover and the Lord's Supper. Tell them the story of the Passover found in Exodus 11 and 12. Help them to see the significance of Jesus instituting the Lord's Supper during Passover as Jesus Himself was preparing to be the sacrifice on the cross, the Lamb of God. An excellent reference book concerning the Passover is Zola Levitt's *The Miracle of Passover.* (You can order a copy from Zola Levitt Ministries, P. O. Box 12268, Dallas, Texas, 75225.)

Resurrection Story

Just before dinner, gather all of the guests to the table. Designate one guest to read or tell the resurrection story of Jesus. Consider allowing the oldest child to present the story, if he or she is at a good reading age. The resurrection account can be found in Matthew 28:1–8; Mark 16:1–8; Luke 24:1–12;

or John 20:1-31. Read it in a "easy to understand" version for the sake of the younger ones. Lead a prayer of thankfulness to God for what He has done for us and enjoy a wonderful meal together using the menu included.

Easter Menu

Fruit Salad in Delicious Baskets
Cola-Baked Brisket
Rosemary New Potatoes
Spring Asparagus Amandine
Citrus Carrots
Easter Rolls
Angel Sherbert Cake

How to Plan This Meal Around Church

With a little preplanning, this meal can be ready in thirty minutes after returning home from Easter morning services. During the thirty minutes of preparation, ask another host or hostess to entertain the children with the predinner activities listed above.

On the Saturday before Easter, make the baskets for the fruit salad. Your children may enjoy helping in this preparation. Slice berries and oranges ahead of time and place in an airtight container, so that you need only add banana slices on Sunday. Prepare the Angel Cake on Friday or Saturday before Easter.

For the Rosemary New Potatoes, wash potatoes and prepare the onion and lemon juice mixture on Saturday. When you return home from church on Sunday, this will be the first item you will assemble so that it can be baking as you prepare the muffins and salad baskets.

Almonds for the asparagus can be toasted ahead of time, and asparagus can be washed Sunday morning to hasten later preparation. Prepare, marinate, and refrigerate brisket on Saturday night so that on Sunday morning it is ready to be popped in the oven.

Fruit Salad in Delicious Baskets

4 cups fresh seasonal berries, with a few Tbsp of sugar
2 bananas, sliced and soaked in orange juice
2 oranges, peeled and sliced

Combine fruit for the fruit salad.
Basket:

½ cup butter or margarine   ½ cup brown sugar (firmly packed)
½ cup light corn syrup   8 Tbsp all-purpose flour
1 cup finely chopped pecans 2 tsp vanilla

❖ Melt butter over low heat. Add brown sugar and corn syrup.
  Cook over high heat, stirring constantly until liquid boils;
  remove from heat and stir in flour and nuts until blended.
  Next, stir in vanilla. Grease and flour baking sheets (make
  sure they are not warped). Place 2–3 Tbsp of batter, about
  8 inches apart (you may only be able to bake two or three
  on a sheet). If the batter does not easily flow, you may need
  to spread or press it out into about a four-inch circle using
  a large spoon or spatula. Bake at 325° for about 12 minutes
  or until they look golden brown.
❖ Cool on a wire rack for a little over one minute until it
  firms up slightly. When just firm enough to lift, loosen
  edges and slide spatula under entire cookie. It should be still
  hot and flexible. Place the cookie on an upside-down wax
  paper cup (2 inches in diameter) and use your hands to
  gently mold it into a basket. Allow basket to cool for 2 minutes
  and then carefully remove from the cup. Repeat the same
  process for each basket, greasing and flouring the baking
  sheets each time.
❖ Baskets can be carefully stored in airtight containers at room
  temperature for up to a week or frozen for longer storage.
❖ Serve fruit salad on a small bed of grated lettuce in the cup.
  Top with whipped cream if you so desire.
❖ Yields about 8 baskets.

Cola-Baked Brisket

1 4–6 lb boneless beef brisket
1 onion, sliced   salt and pepper
1 can diet or regular cola   1 garlic clove minced

❖ Place sliced onions in bottom of roasting pan. Sprinkle both
  sides of brisket with salt and pepper and place, fat side up,
  on top of the onions. Prick brisket several times with fork.

Slowly pour cola over brisket. Season with garlic and cover with aluminum foil. Bake at 325 for 4–4½ hours, basting occasionally. Serve on large platter; garnish with onions.

Rosemary New Potatoes

25–30 small thin-skinned red potatoes, scrubbed
  ½ cup minced red onion   2 Tbsp lemon juice
  ¾ cup olive oil   salt
 6–8 sprigs fresh rosemary or   2 tsp dry rosemary

❖ Combine minced onions and lemon juice and set aside. Arrange potatoes in a single layer in a shallow 9 x 13 pan. Pour oil around the potatoes. Stir in onion/lemon juice mixture and top with about 4 sprigs of fresh rosemary or dry herbs.

❖ Bake at 400° for about 25–35 minutes, stirring potatoes occasionally to rotate them in oil. Using a large pronged fork, prick large potatoes to check for doneness. Salt to taste. Garnish with additional rosemary and serve in a large serving bowl.

❖ Yields 8–10 servings.

Spring Asparagus Amandine

  ¾ cup slivered blanched almonds
  3 lbs asparagus
  ¼ cup butter or margarine   ½ tsp salt

❖ Toast almonds in large skillet using two Tbsp of butter over medium heat until golden. Remove almonds to a small plate and set aside. Cut the tough base off of the end of the asparagus. Steam asparagus until tender-crisp and color is bright. Pour melted butter over the top and sprinkle with salt and toasted almonds.

❖ Yields 12 servings.

Citrus Carrots

35–40 mini-carrots, washed and skinned
  3 Tbsp orange juice

❖ Steam mini-carrots until slightly tender. Gently toss in orange juice. Garnish with parsley.

❖ Yields 10–12 servings.

Easter Rolls

2 cups self-rising flour
2 cups vanilla ice cream, softened

❖ Lightly stir ingredients together until just moistened.
❖ Line mini-muffin tins with paper liners. Fill ¾ full. Bake 20
   minutes at 325°.
❖ Yields: 16–20 muffins.

You may want to tell the symbolism of these biscuits during dinner. The biscuits are unique because they require only two ingredients. It reminds me of Jesus who was made of two different ingredients, both man and God. Jesus called Himself the "Bread of Life." Yeast in the Bible is referred to as sin, but there was no sin in Jesus, just as there is no yeast in this bread.

The flour used in this recipe is "self-rising" flour. Although several people in the Bible rose from the dead (Lazarus, the widow's son, Jairus' daughter), Jesus was the only one who was *self*-rising. We, too, have victory over sin and death. In addition to all of this symbolism, the rolls themselves look like the stone that was rolled away from the tomb!

Angel Sherbet Cake

1 loaf angel food or sponge cake
1 quart sherbet, any flavor

❖ Place sherbet in refrigerator, allowing it to soften but not become liquid. Slice cake in half horizontally and set both slices in the freezer for about an hour to harden and ease preparation. Place one layer of cake on a serving plate and spread evenly with 2 cups of sherbet. Top with remaining cake layer. Quickly spoon and spread remaining sherbet over top of the cake. Cover and freeze overnight.
❖ When serving, let stand at room temperature for about 5 minutes before slicing. Cut slices about 1½ inches thick and garnish with fresh fruit.
❖ Yields 10–12 servings

After-Dinner Fellowship

The time after dinner can be a relaxed time of fellowship, enjoying a cup of coffee or tea together and reflecting on the day. Here are a few extra ideas to consider incorporating to the celebration.

Easter Egg Roll

In your backyard or nearby grassy area, designate a start and end for this special race. You will need hard-boiled eggs (one per person) and sticks (yardsticks, broomsticks, or tree branches). Each person lines up behind the starting line with egg and stick. When the "Go" signal is given, each player must roll his egg to the finish using their stick. The person who rolls his egg over the finish line first, wins.

For younger kids, award a prize to everyone who finishes.

Singing Celebration

If you have a musician in the group, or if most of your guests enjoy singing, then plan a time of worship through song.

Seed Planting Ceremony

Provide several packages of seeds and ask your guests to join you in the garden, or potential garden, and plant the seeds together. Read and discuss the parable of the "Sower and the Seeds" found in Matthew 13:1–23.

Final Note

Some family members who join you for this celebration may not be believers. This is a special time for them to see and experience God's love. Be sensitive to your guests and their comfort level (for instance, nonbelievers would not necessarily understand or enjoy singing praises to God or praying out loud). Create an atmosphere of warmth and love for your guests on this day and allow God to draw them to Himself.

> "And I, if I am lifted up from the earth, will draw all peoples to Myself."
>
> JOHN 12:32

SUMMERTIME PICNIC

SUMMERTIME SCHEDULE • 2-4 HOURS

1-1.5 Hours:	*Snacks and arrival games*
40 Minutes:	*Picnic lunch*
1-1.5 Hours:	*Large group games*

The length of this picnic depends on your group's intention and purpose. As the host of the event, keep a loose schedule of activities. Games in this chapter are listed in two categories (Arrival Games and Large Group Games) and can be mixed or rearranged as you desire.

Church fellowships, Fourth of July celebrations, family reunions, Labor Day outings, back-to-school parties—no matter what type of occasion you are planning, beat the heat with this summertime treat! Outdoor games galore will provide loads of fun for both adults and children. Top it all off with a tasty picnic lunch and refreshing cold drinks.

Picnic Basket Invitations

You can cut a simple picnic basket invitation out of brown poster board and draw crisscross lines on the side of the basket using a black marker. Cut a small triangle of red-and-white-checked fabric and attach it to the back of the invitation, allowing a small portion to hang over the front. Print the invitation information on white paper and glue it to the back of the basket.

Another idea for invitations is to purchase small, inexpensive Frisbees. Attach the invitation information to the Frisbee and send in a large envelope. Instruct the guests to bring the Frisbee to the picnic. The invitations should read as follows:

FOOD, FUN, AND GAMES!
It's going to be a great time at the
(reason for party) Picnic!
Please join us . . .

Time: _____

Date:_____

Location:_____

RSVP: _____

Looking forward to seeing you there!!

For patriotic themes, use red paper to print your invitation and add gold star stickers or attach an American flag.

Outdoor Decorations

More than likely this picnic gathering will take place at a local park or other outdoor setting. Your decorations, therefore, will be fairly limited. Balloons are an excellent outdoor decoration along with flags. Choose one or two theme colors to coordinate with the purpose of your event. Purchase tablecloths, napkins, and balloons to fit the color scheme. If this is a family reunion, you may want to make several flags displaying the family name or crest. For an official holiday, you may choose red, white, and blue or holiday colors. If this is a back-to-school event, use school colors for flags, pennants, pom-poms, and balloons. Don't forget name tags in the same colors.

Bring a battery-powered cassette or CD player to play your favorite Christian music or perhaps patriotic or beach music. In case of a windy day, pack several bricks or heavy objects to hold down tablecloths and other items that may blow away.

Snacks and Arrival Games

As guests arrive, provide some light snacks to be enjoyed during the opening games. Pretzels, chips, snack mix, or trail mix are good starters. Several five-gallon drink containers plus cups are essentials for this picnic. One should be filled with ice water and the other filled with lemonade. You may want a third container filled with iced tea. Since the picnic involves quite a few active games, and the heat will most likely be a factor, you need to have plenty of thirst-quenching drinks.

Nature Scavenger Hunt

As guests arrive, allow them to go in groups or families to find the items on a nature scavenger hunt. You can make a list judging from your own geographical location or tell the groups to find one item that starts with each letter of the alphabet, excluding Q, X, and Z. Give each team a special bag or basket to collect their items. Provide prizes for finishers or winners. A variation of the scavenger hunt could be a hunt with clues leading to a certain destination.

Goofy Golf

Young and old alike will enjoy a round of Goofy Golf. You can make your own course by using empty cans, wood pegs, baking flour, and several items to create a challenge to the course. You will need nine cans for the course and twenty-seven pegs. Set cans on their side and hammer one peg into the ground on either side of the can so that it cannot roll. Hammer one peg in the ground at the back of the can to help hold it in place.

Mark the pathway to each hole using baking flour poured through a funnel. Put small obstacles in the pathway such as bricks, toys, wood planks, bowls, sand, traffic cones, rope, croquet wickets, or a large can with both ends removed. The object of the game is to putt the ball into the can. Use golf balls and putters. For more of a challenge, use tennis balls and broomsticks. Play as teams, as families, or as individuals. You may want to have prizes for the lowest scores.

Fabulous Flying Frisbees

Provide plenty of Frisbees for both the kids and adults. Guests can toss the discs back and forth, or you may want to create an obstacle course for the Frisbees similar to a golf course. The course can be easily set up by placing small signs numbered 1 to 9 on various objects that are at least ten yards from each other.

Players follow the signs in chronological order, attempting to hit the objects with their Frisbee using the least amount of throws. Add hoops and baskets to make the course more challenging.

One-Legged Water Gun Madness

Here's a fun way for the kids to stay cool (and adults too, if they do not mind getting a little wet). Provide a water gun for each participant. Place a large bucket of water in the center of the area of play. The bucket is for refill purposes. Tell everyone to fill up their gun and get ready for action. There are only two rules to the game. Rule One: All participants must be hopping on one foot. Rule Two: They may not shoot at anyone's face (violation of this rule means confiscation of weapon). Players must hold their water guns in one hand and one of their feet in the other hand while hopping around trying to squirt the other players. The refill bucket is the one "safe" place.

Data Processing Dilemma

This is a good game to help your guests get to know one another. Call out a data topic, such as first names, last names, birth places, street numbers, birthday months, shoe size, hair length, etc. Players then must move as fast as possible to place themselves in alphabetical, chronological, or numerical order. Much information will be shared, and by the end of the game everyone should know a little more about one another.

You can play a slightly different version of this game by grouping together with others who share the same characteristics. Call out a category such as hair color and everyone groups together according to hair colors. Begin with obvious characteristics—shoe color, eye color, shorts, or long pants—then move to categories that reveal something about the people, such as favorite ice cream flavor (vanilla, chocolate, or strawberry), birth location (north, south, east, or west), favorite books (fiction, nonfiction), and on and on.

Larger-Than-Life Pickup Sticks

Visit a hardware store and purchase a dozen or more yardsticks.

(Some hardware stores give yardsticks away free of charge.) Several days before the picnic, spray-paint the sticks. Using four different colors, paint at least three sticks in each color.

Participants may play as individuals or as a team. Jumble the sticks in a pile on the ground. A color is assigned to each team or person. Each player on his turn attempts to get one of his colored sticks out of the pile without disturbing the other sticks. If he does make another stick move, then he forfeits his turn. The first player to retrieve all of his sticks is the winner.

Giant Chair
Gather young and old together in a circle. They must stand shoulder to shoulder. Tell participants to turn to their right (be sure to help younger ones go in the right direction). On the count of three, everyone is to slowly sit on the knees of the person in back of them. If this is done properly, everyone should be sitting fairly comfortably. If it doesn't work the first time, try, try again.

Bubblemania
Provide a variety of bubble-making objects. Use store-bought bubble formula or make your own. Even the adults can enter into the fun with contests for the largest bubble, the longest lasting bubble, and the highest flying bubble.

Homemade Bubble Formula

1 cup water	½ cup dishwashing liquid
¼ cup glycerin	¼ cup corn syrup

❖ Stir ingredients together. Bubble makers can be made from straws, cardboard rolls, cookie cutters, or shaped coat hangers.

Picnic Menu
Multicolored Pasta Salad
Ham and Swiss Circle Sandwiches
Fresh Fruit
Sesame Breadsticks
Butterscotch Chocolate Squares

You can choose one of two ways to serve the picnic meal. Either provide plates and napkins to serve buffet-style or provide small baskets or boxes for individual prepacked meals. Use produce baskets (quart size) with a decorative napkin for a lovely but inexpensive individual meal basket.

Multicolored Pasta Salad

1 (8 oz) pkg multicolored corkscrew pasta
3 medium carrots, peeled and diced
2 stalks of celery, diced
1 medium onion, peeled and chopped
1 medium cucumber, peeled and chopped
1 large tomato, peeled and chopped
½ cup vegetable oil   ½ cup cider vinegar
⅓ cup sugar   1 tsp salt
½ tsp pepper

❖ Cook pasta according to package directions; drain. Rinse with cold water; drain again. Combine pasta, carrots, celery, onion, cucumber, and tomato. Combine remaining ingredients in a jar and shake to mix well. Pour dressing over pasta and vegetable mixture and toss gently. Cover and chill for 8 hours. Serve in small plastic covered containers or cups.
❖ Yields: 6–8 servings.

Ham and Swiss Circle Sandwiches

¾ cup mayonnaise   3 Tbsp sweet pickle relish
1½ Tbsp Dijon mustard
12 slices, white, wheat, or rye bread, toasted
12 (1 oz) slices ham   12 (1 oz) slices Swiss cheese
6 lettuce leaves, washed and dried

❖ Mix first three ingredients. Spread mayonnaise mixture on one side of each slice of bread. Top half of bread slices with 2 slices ham, 2 slices cheese, and lettuce leaf. Cover with remaining bread slices. Use large round cookie cutter to cut sandwiches into circles. Be sure to keep sandwiches in cooler until ready to serve. Cut in half for smaller sandwiches for young ones.
❖ Yields 6 large circle sandwiches.

Fresh Fruit

Provide seasonal fresh fruit in each basket or on the buffet table. Several strawberries or clusters of grapes look good on the side. Depending on how fancy you want to be for this picnic, you could serve the fruit in orange cups. Cut a small slice from the ends of each fruit so that they will sit level. Cut the oranges in half using a zigzag cut. Scoop out the pulp to create a small serving bowl.

Sesame Breadsticks

¾ cup butter or margarine, softened
2 cups all-purpose flour   1 tsp salt
2 dashes cayenne pepper   1 cup sesame seeds
   salt   ice water

❖ Cut butter into flour mixed with salt and cayenne pepper. Sprinkle ice water over dough and toss with a fork until dough holds together. Roll dough out on a floured board to ⅛ inch thickness and cut into 1 x 3 strips. Place on an ungreased cookie sheet, sprinkle generously with sesame seeds, and bake at 325° for about 15 minutes. Before removing from pan and while still hot, sprinkle with a little salt. May be frozen for later use (thaw to room temperature and bake).

❖ Yields about 4 dozen sticks.

Butterscotch Chocolate Squares

½ cup butter or margarine, softened to room temp
2 cups packed brown sugar   3 eggs
1 tsp vanilla extract   2 Tbsp grated orange peel
¼ tsp salt   2½ cups all-purpose flour
2 tsp baking powder   ¾ cup chopped walnuts
1 cup semisweet chocolate pieces
1 cup butterscotch flavored pieces

❖ Beat together butter, brown sugar, eggs, vanilla, orange peel, and salt until light and fluffy. Add flour and baking powder, beating until blended. Stir in the last three ingredients. Spread batter evenly in a 15 x 10 jellyroll pan lined with foil. Bake at 350° for 20–25 minutes or until golden brown. Cool in pan. Cut into bars when cool. Wrap two bars together in colored cellophane and keep in coolers until serving time.

❖ Yields about 40 bars.

Large Group Activities

Softball and soccer are two sports that most ages and athletic levels can enjoy together. Here are some basic guidelines for both sports as well as several fun and unique variations.

Softball

Softball is essentially the same as baseball with the exception of a lighter bat and larger, softer core ball. Most of the rules are identical to baseball except for two: (1) the pitcher is limited to an underhand throw, (2) a base runner must remain in contact with his base until the pitcher starts his pitch.

Standard softball consists of seven innings. You may want to consider some of these general rules to keep the game fair among average players.

- No permanent pitcher, each team changes pitchers every inning. (This prevents the game being dominated by the pitcher.)
- No bunting.
- No cleated shoes.
- No windmill windup.

Softball variations include:

Crossout Softball. Played the same as standard softball except that a fielder may put a base runner out by throwing the ball across his path ahead of him. The ball must pass between the runner and the base toward which he is running.

Single Score Softball. Whenever a batter hits a fair ball, he runs the bases as in regular softball and earns a point for his team for each base he reaches. If he makes it to second base and then is out as he runs to third, he still has earned two points for his team. A home run is worth 4 points.

Hand Softball. Same rules as softball except that a tennis ball or other light ball is used and the batter strikes it with his hand or fist.

Volley Softball. No pitching in this game, rather the batter serves a volley ball. The ball must cross a line 15 feet ahead in order to be in play. The game continues with the same rules as softball.

Throwball. Same as softball only without a pitcher or bat. The batter stands at home and throws the ball, then runs.

Soccer

The object of soccer is to kick the ball into the opposing team's goal. At the beginning of each period and after each score, play is started with a kickoff. When the ball goes out of bounds, it is kicked or thrown in by an opponent of the players who last touched it, as in basketball. If the ball goes across the sideline, then it is thrown in from outside the line—both feet on the ground and hand over head toss. If the ball is driven across the goal line, but not between the goal posts by the attacking side, the ball is kicked into the field of play from beyond the goal line. If the ball is kicked across the goal line by the defending team, the attacking team takes a "corner kick" by kicking the ball into the field from the nearer of the two corners. Play four 15-minute quarters or shorten the quarters considering the ages and abilities of the players.

Soccer variations:

Chaseball. Same rules as soccer except players are allowed to hit the ball with their fists.

Mass Soccer. This version of soccer is played with large numbers of players, perhaps twenty-five to a team. General rules apply although the game is played with more than one ball. You may want to add up to four balls in play at one time. You will need at least two goalkeepers instead of one.

Line Soccer. Both teams form a line on their own half of the field ten yards from the middle line. Each player extends his arms behind the backs of those on either side, joining hands with the person second from him. The ball is placed at center field. At the signal both teams rush forward to kick the ball. The line must not be broken. If it breaks, play is stopped, the ball is moved ten yards toward the offender's goal, and the game restarts from the new position. A goal is scored when a team kicks the ball across the opponent's goal line. No goal posts are needed.

SPECIAL NOTE: Don't forget to pack a first-aid kit for any unexpected injuries!

Party Additions and Variations

If this is an Independence Day celebration, invite families with small children to bring along the children's bicycles for a parade. Supply crepe paper and streamers to decorate the bikes. Guide the parade of decorated vehicles on a short ride around the park or down the sidewalk. Also, take time to read or tell stories of our founding fathers and their struggle for independence to provide freedom for us all. Ask a veteran of the armed forces to share with your guests about his or her experiences.

Instead of a picnic you can easily make this party into a barbecue dinner (see chap. 7 for menu ideas). Or consider hosting a BYOM (Bring Your Own Meat) cookout in which you ask your guests to bring their favorite meat to the cookout, and you provide the grills and the side dishes.

Final Note

This is a light-hearted and fun outing. Keep it that way! Do not allow stiff or brutal competition to get in the way of a relaxing and fun activity. Mix teams as you play each new activity; smile and encourage sportsmanship. Prizes can be bags of candy or packs of gum. Provide enough so that the winning team can share with the other team.

> Walk in a manner worthy of the calling with which you have been called, with all humility and gentleness, with patience, showing forbearance to one another in love, being diligent to preserve the unity of the Spirit in the bond of peace.
>
> EPHESIANS 4:1–3

Chapter 20

THANKSGIVING FEAST

SCHEDULE
Thanksgiving Day should not be tied to a schedule.

"Oh, give thanks to the LORD, for He is good!"
(Ps. 106:1). Thanksgiving is a wonderful time of year
to show our gratefulness to the Lord. You will find
this feast focuses on the Father and not just the food.
Consider inviting someone who does not have
family members nearby. Your entire family will be
blessed by special guests at this faith-building feast.

"Corny" Invitations

Although formal invitations are not necessary for Thanksgiving dinner, a thoughtful card and reminder of the arrival time is a nice idea and adds to the anticipation of the gathering. Using a fine point brown paint pen, write the invitation information on deep orange card-stock stationery. Glue several kernels of Indian corn onto the card at the side of the information. The invitation reads as follows:

> "Oh, give thanks to the LORD, for He is good!
> For His mercy endures forever."—PSALM 136:1

> Please join us in a celebration of
> ## *Thanksgiving*

Arrival Time: _____

Address: _____

(Include the date if you think it is necessary)

Pilgrim and Native American Decorations

Cornucopias and baskets full of harvest vegetables and gourds will make wonderful decorations throughout your home. For the front door, tie three ears of Indian corn together at the base of the husks with autumn-colored ribbons. Attach to the door as you would a wreath. Use parchment paper to print a scroll reading, "In everything give thanks; for this is the will of God in Christ Jesus for you. 1 Thessalonians 5:18," and attach to the door as well.

Inside, the smell of roasted turkey and all of the trimmings will fill the air with a wonderful scent. For background music visit your local Christian bookstore to find a tape or CD containing songs of praise and thanksgiving. Pilgrim figurines are available at decorative stores. You may be able to find Pilgrim candle holders, salt and pepper shakers, tea pots, and napkin rings to enhance the look of your home and dinner table.

For the table centerpiece, use a lovely cornucopia basket or a pumpkin (gutted and cleaned) filled with squash, small pumpkins, gourds, and Indian corn or a dried floral arrangement. The centerpiece should be easy to move in case you want to place the turkey at the center of the table at dinnertime. For place cards, use harvest-colored cards with five kernels of corn glued to each card beside the names. Before or during dinner you will be sharing the story of the five kernels of corn with your guests. If children are involved in the celebration, they can add to the decorations through several predinner craft activities listed later in the chapter.

Use your everyday plates or china for the dinner (although plastic or paper is a good idea for young kids). If you see that the dinner table is going to be too crowded, serve the food buffet-style from a separate location, allowing more room at the eating table. Separate tables for adults and children is a possibility, although I personally try to go to great lengths to include children at the same table as the adults for Thanksgiving since this is a holiday filled with family togetherness.

Thanksgiving Gathering

This should be a relaxing day full of food, thanksgiving, and fellowship. I suggest that you provide predinner activities for the children to keep them occupied while the dinner is in its final preparation. I have listed several ideas below.

Arrival

As guests arrive, it is a good idea to share the responsibility of greeting with your spouse or another family member. Ask everyone to sign the Thankfulness Board. This is a lovely orange poster board, decorated with Thanksgiving stickers or drawings as a border. At the top of the poster is written, "I will give Thee thanks with all my heart. Psalm 138:1." Each guest is to write on the board something for which they are thankful and sign their name.

During the arrival time, the cooks in the family generally join together in the kitchen for food preparation, while the others enjoy talking, watching the football games, or other activities. Set out a jigsaw puzzle or start a board game. Some may enjoy playing a basketball game in the driveway or a type of yard game if it is nice weather.

Snacks and Punch

It is also helpful to provide simple snacks and punch before dinner for hungry appetites. Crackers and a cheese ball, plus some celery and carrot sticks will do the trick. For older kids and adults set out a bowl of assorted nuts and a nut cracker, but be sure to keep these out reach of the little ones.

Thanksgiving Punch

1	quart water	3–4	regular tea bags
1	cup sugar	1	cup freshly squeezed lemon juice
2	cups orange juice	3	cups cranberry juice
2	cups water		Ice cubes
2	cups ginger ale	1	sliced lemon
2	sliced limes		Several Maraschino cherries

❖ Bring 1 quart water to a full rolling boil. Remove from heat and add tea bags; steep for 5 minutes. Remove bags and set aside to cool at room temperature. Combine with sugar, fruit juices, and 2 cups water. Pour into a large container and chill. Just before serving pour into a punch bowl. Add ice cubes and ginger ale. Garnish with lemon and lime slices and cherries.

❖ Yields: 10–15 servings.

Predinner Children's Crafts

Purchase and prepare for the children's craft several days in advance. Assign a teenager or adult to help supervise these fun activities on the day of the event while you are busy in the kitchen.

Orange Turkey Gobbler (ages 3–10). You will need a box of tooth picks, a bag of soft gumdrops, brown and red construction paper, and oranges (one per child). The orange will serve as the body of the turkey. The large tail of the turkey is created from toothpicks loaded with gumdrops. Stick the toothpicks in a fan-like array for the tail. The head of the turkey is made from brown construction paper, adding a little red paper at the bottom of the head for the gobbler. Glue or tape the construction paper head to a toothpick and put the head in the orange, opposite the tail. Use three toothpicks in the bottom of the orange to help the turkey stand. These make special table decorations or place card holders.

Native American Beads and Vests (ages 3–8). Provide beads and string for the kids to create beaded necklaces, reminding them of the kindness of the Native Americans and the important part they played in the first Thanksgiving. Children also can decorate and wear Native American vests. Use grocery sacks with holes cut out for the arms and head and a slit down the front center. You also can purchase tan or light brown fabric remnants and cut them into simple vests. Use markers to decorate the vests with Native American patterns and symbols. Allow kids to decorate strips of leather and then add a feather to make a headband.

Pilgrim Hats (ages 3–8). Each of the girls can make their own Pilgrim hat by simply taking a 12 x 18 piece of white paper and folding back the 11-inch side to make a 1½-inch margin. Take the unfolded corners and roll them together to form the back of the hat. Staple to secure.

Boys can make tall black hats with large rims and a belt buckle on the front. You will need a large piece of black construction paper rolled into a pipe approximately 6 inches in diameter. Cut an 8-inch circle with a 6-inch hole for the rim of the hat and tape to the top portion from inside. Use a small rectangle of yellow paper glued to the front of the hat for the buckle. The children can use these items for costumes in the after-dinner play about the first Thanksgiving.

First Thanksgiving Proclamation

Just before dinner, gather everyone together and allow one person (perhaps the oldest child of reading age) to read the First Thanksgiving Proclamation. In 1789 George Washington made this statement:

> "Whereas it is the duty of all nations to acknowledge the providence of Almighty God, to obey His will, to be grateful for His benefits, and humbly implore His protection, aid and favors . . .
>
> "Now, therefore, I do recommend and assign Thursday the 26th day of November next, to be devoted by the people of these states to the service of that great and glorious Being, who is the Beneficent Author of all the good that was, that is, or that will be, that we may then all unite in rendering unto Him our sincere and humble thanks for His kind care and protection of the people of this country, and for all the great and various favors which He has been pleased to confer upon us."[1]

After reading the proclamation, allow another guest to read the expressions of gratitude written on the Thankfulness

Board by all of the guests. After the reading, join hands and give thanks for not only the food but for the many blessings that you have experienced in the past year. One person can lead the prayer (preferably the head of the household) or allow everyone to pray if they so desire.

The story of the first Thanksgiving and the five kernels of corn is a significant story to tell year after year to your guests. You can either tell the story before dinner or as everyone enjoys their food. A longer version of the story can be found in the book *The Light and the Glory* by Peter Marshall and David Manuel (Grand Rapids, Mich.: Fleming H. Revel Company, 1977).

Story of Thanksgiving and the Five Kernels of Corn

Journey with me back to the first winter that the Pilgrims experienced at Plymouth. It was a difficult year. With disease, very little food, and poor shelter, many died that horrible winter. Yet the harder the circumstances, the more the Pilgrims prayed and trusted in God's help. In the following spring, God miraculously provided two English-speaking Native Americans, Samoset and Squanto. These men not only brought the Pilgrims and neighboring Native Americans together in a friendly relationship, but they also helped teach the Pilgrims how to farm the land.

Squanto stayed with the Pilgrims, teaching them how to plant corn, stalk deer, plant pumpkins, and make maple syrup. He also taught them about herbs for cooking and medicine and helped them to learn the beaver trade. William Bradford wrote in his diary that Squanto was a "true gift from God."

By fall, the Pilgrims had a bountiful fold of crops to help them through the winter. Governor Bradford declared a day of public thanksgiving to God for the crops and for the Native Americans. The festivities with the Native Americans lasted three days as they feasted and played games. Unfortunately, the coming winter brought another "starving time." The Pilgrims had new settlers who had joined them and their supplies depleted quickly. At one point they were down to daily rations of five kernels of corn a piece. By God's grace, an unexpected ship came into harbor from Virginia. The captain traded food for beaver pelts. The Pilgrims now had food to make it through the winter.

The next year, the Pilgrims knew that they needed twice as much corn to feed the growing colony, so they faithfully planted more than enough. Unbelievably, a twelve-week drought came in the summer leaving the crops limp and almost dead. The Pilgrims knew that there was only one thing to do and that was to go to God with their need. The Pilgrims declared a day of fasting and prayer. They gathered in the common blockhouse in the morning and began praying. They spent many hours in prayer and praise to God. By the time they left, dark clouds were forming in the sky. The next day a soft sweet rain began to fall, lasting for fourteen days. The Pilgrims harvested all the crops they needed that year to last them through the winter.

At the second thanksgiving celebration both Native Americans and Pilgrims together thanked God for ending the drought. The Native Americans recognized God's mighty hand in the provision of rain as they observed the Pilgrims' prayers being answered. All participants enjoyed another festival of food and games, but at each place setting lay five kernels of corn as a reminder of God's loving care.

Thanksgiving Dinner Menu

Kinder Cranberry Salad
Roasted Turkey with Citrus Glaze
Squash Dressing in Squash Bowls
Aunt Mary Sue's Sweet Potatoes
Green Bean Amandine
Pan-Baked Yeast Rolls
Pumpkin Pie Supreme

Share the Thanksgiving responsibilities with your guests so that everyone has a part in preparing the feast. Allow your children to help you as well. I love to show my daughters the Thanksgiving menu selection and let each of them choose one item to help prepare for the dinner. They take pleasure in being a part of the preparation process and feel a sense of accomplishment (especially when someone compliments their dish!).

Kinder Cranberry Salad

1 (3 oz) pkg raspberry gelatin
1 (16 oz) can whole cranberries
1 (8 oz) can crushed pineapple
¾ cup chopped pecans
1 (8 oz) tub of whipped cream (low fat is fine)

❖ Drain pineapple, reserving juice. Add water to juice to make almost a cup. Bring to a boil. Remove from heat and stir in gelatin until dissolved. Add cranberries and pineapple. Chill until firm but not set. Fold in whipped cream and nuts. Pour into 9 x 13 glass pan, cover and refrigerate until congealed.
❖ Yields 12 servings.

Roasted Turkey with Citrus Glaze

3 Tbsp oil
salt and pepper
1 garlic clove, minced
1 tsp dried thyme leaves
1 large onion
1 8–12 lb turkey

❖ Set oven to 325°. Prepare thawed turkey, cleaning inside and out. Brush turkey on all sides with oil, then rub with thyme leaves; sprinkle with salt and pepper. Place onion and garlic inside turkey cavity and place bird in roasting pan. Make a tent over the bird using aluminum foil and cook as directed (approximately 4¾–5½ hours). Test doneness by moving drumstick up and down. Leg joint should give readily or break. Meat thermometer inserted into thigh should read 200°.

Citrus Glaze

¾ cup orange marmalade
½ cup frozen orange juice concentrate, thawed
2 Tbsp margarine   ½ tsp ginger

❖ Combine ingredients in a small saucepan and cook over medium heat, stirring constantly until smooth.

❖ When turkey is done, remove from oven and brush with glaze. Let turkey stand 15 minutes before carving. Pour remaining glaze into a gravy dish to spoon over turkey servings.

❖ Yeilds 6–8 servings.

Squash Dressing in Squash Bowls

10–12 medium yellow squash	1 small onion, chopped
1 tsp minced garlic	⅓ cup chopped celery
1 (8 oz) pkg herb-seasoned stuffing	
½ cup margarine	

❖ Steam squash along with onion, garlic, and celery until tender. Drain and put in large bowl. Melt butter and pour over vegetables. Add stuffing and mix. Put in 9 x 13 casserole dish and bake at 350° for 30 minutes. This dressing is a delicious complement to your turkey dinner. Although it is not necessary, you may enjoy serving the dressing in squash bowls if you want to go the extra mile.

❖ Yields 10–12 servings.

Squash Bowls:

Acorn squash (one per guest)   oil and water

❖ Cut off top third of each squash. Scrape out pulp from the bottom of the squash. Brush insides with oil to prevent the squash from drying out. Place squash in roasting pan with ¼ cup of water in the bottom of the pan and bake 350° for 40 minutes. Remove squash from oven and cover with aluminum foil to keep warm. Spoon cooked dressing into squash bowls. Cover and keep warm until serving.

Aunt Mary Sue's Sweet Potatoes

3 cups sweet potatoes (4 large potatoes, cooked and mashed)	
½ cup sugar	½ cup butter
2 eggs, beaten	1 tsp vanilla
⅓ cup milk	

Combine all ingredients and pour into a greased casserole dish.

Topping:

⅓ cup melted butter	1 cup light brown sugar
½ cup flour	1 cup pecans, chopped

❖ Combine topping ingredients and pour over potato mixture. Bake at 350° for about 35–45 minutes.
❖ Yields 10–12 servings.

Green Bean Amandine

3 lbs fresh green beans	1 cup slivered almonds
½ cup butter	salt
1 lemon	

❖ Steam cut green beans until crisp. Melt butter in large sauce pan, add almonds just before pouring over green beans. Salt to taste.
❖ Serve with twisted lemon slices as garnish.
❖ Yields 10–12 servings.

Pan Baked Yeast Rolls

2 pkg dry yeast	⅔ cup sugar, divided
1 cup warm water	1 tsp salt
½ cup butter or margarine	½ cup shortening
1 cup boiling water	2 eggs, beaten
6–7 cups all-purpose flour, divided	

❖ Dissolve yeast and 1 tsp sugar in 1 cup warm water; let stand about 5 minutes. Combine remaining sugar, salt, butter, and shortening in a large bowl. Add boiling water, stirring until butter and shortening melt. Cool slightly.
❖ Add dissolved yeast, stirring well. Add eggs and 3 cups flour, beating at medium speed of an electric mixer until smooth. Gradually stir in enough remaining flour to make a soft dough. Place in a well-greased bowl, turning to grease top. Cover and let rise in a warm place (85°), free from drafts, 1–1½ hours or until doubled in bulk.
❖ Punch down dough; turn dough out onto a well-floured surface, and knead several times. Shape into 2-inch balls, and place in 3 greased 9-inch round pans. Cover and let rise in a warm place, free from drafts, 30–40 minutes or until doubled in size. Bake at 325° for 20–25 minutes until golden.

Pumpkin Pie Supreme

2 eggs, beaten	1 (16 oz) can pumpkin
1 cup firmly packed brown sugar	
1 tsp cinnamon	½ tsp nutmeg
½ tsp ginger	¼ tsp cloves
1 Tbsp flour	½ tsp salt
1 (14 oz) can sweetened condensed milk	
1 9-inch pastry pie shell (unbaked)	

❖ Combine eggs and pumpkin. Blend in sugar, spices, flour, and salt; mix well. Add milk and mix. Pour into pastry pie shell. Bake at 425° for 15 minutes. Reduce heat to 350° and continue baking for 35–40 minutes or until knife inserted near center comes out clean. Cool.

❖ Yields 8 servings.

After-Dinner Fellowship

After dinner take a family walk, finish the jigsaw puzzle, play another board game, watch more football, or play a friendly game of kickball, soccer, or football in the yard. Some may want to take a nap after the big meal while others work together in the kitchen for cleanup duty. Encourage the children to act out the story of the Pilgrims and the early Thanksgiving stories of the five kernels of corn. The adults will make an excellent audience.

Final Note

Being together with extended and immediate family members can be a special time for some and a difficult time for others. Family members can hit our sensitivity button more so than most people. Perhaps there are family members with whom you have a hard time getting along. This may be a good time to ask God to help heal that wound and let His love work through you. A big part of getting along with others is over-looking their shortcomings and forgetting past wrongs. We all need to have feathers like a duck's back—letting grievances, shortcomings, and comments roll right off of us.

Keep in mind that although forgiveness is a difficult thing, God desires for us to forgive others as He has forgiven us. On this Thanksgiving Day we can be most thankful that God allowed His only Son to give His life so our sins could be forgiven. Shouldn't we in turn forgive others?

> And so, as those who have been chosen of God, holy and beloved, put on a heart of compassion, kindness, humility, gentleness and patience; bearing with one another, and forgiving each other, whoever has a complaint against anyone; just as the Lord forgave you, so also should you. And beyond all these things put on love, which is the perfect bond of unity. And let the peace of Christ rule in your hearts, to which indeed you were called in one body; and be thankful.
>
> COLOSSIANS 3:12–15, NASB

---

1. *A Compilation of the Messages and Papers of the Presidents 1789–1902*, 11 vols., John D. Richardson, ed. (Washington, D.C.: Bureau of National Literature and Art, 1907).

Chapter 21

CHRISTMAS TEA

TEA SCHEDULE • 1.5 HOURS	
50 Minutes:	Arrival, tea and goodies, chat
15 Minutes:	Symbols of the Season
25 Minutes:	Continued talk or sharing

Enjoy a relaxing spot of tea with friends amidst the hustle and bustle of the holidays! Delicious scones, finger sandwiches, and cookies will accompany tea and Christmas Punch. Make this an opportunity to share Christ's love using the "Symbols of the Season" in a brief message included in this chapter. What a wonderful time of the year to share the good news of Jesus with friends, neighbors, and family.

Tea Invitations

For Christmas Tea invitations, use holiday note cards with a seasonal border. You may write your own invitations using lovely handwriting or calligraphy, or consider taking them to a printer. The wording is as follows:

As a cup of tea warms the body,
So friendship warms the heart.
You are invited to an informal
Christmas Tea
on (day of week), December_____

*4:00 to 5:30 in the Afternoon
(_____ address _____)
RSVP: (___ name and number ___)

   *Traditional time for tea is four o'clock, and usually lasts 1½ to 2 hours. It seems today that tea is served anytime in between the hours of three and six. Be sure to state a definite starting and ending time on your invitation.

Decorations

More than likely your home is already decorated for the holidays, so I will focus on decorating ideas for the tea buffet table. Use a lace or white linen tablecloth. Napkins may be white cloth or fancy paper. Some ladies enjoy collecting antique embroidered napkins from estate and garage sales. This would be a lovely occasion to use a variety of special napkins.

   Use your china dessert plates and cups and/or your Christmas china. If you have more guests than you have cups and plates, use paper plates with a white lace doily on top or borrow extra china. Again, you may enjoy collecting a variety of china cups and saucers from different sales. A wide array of patterns add color and beauty to the tea service. Feel free to mix different patterns if you need to borrow from family and friends.

Table Arrangement

Cinnamon, apple, or cranberry create lovely scents for the Christmas season. Use simmering potpourri or candles to create the desired aroma. Instrumental Christmas music should be softly playing during the tea, preferably classical selections. For name tags use white tags, adding white lace ribbon around the edges; or use holiday name tags readily available at party supply stores.

   Utilize two rooms for tea, one for the food and tea presentation (buffet-style), and one for the guests to gather and enjoy their plates of food and tea. Place a tray with tea service at one end of the table and a punch bowl at the opposite end. In the middle of the buffet table provide an assortment of finger foods as well as mints and nuts. Napkins, cups, and saucers should be placed just to the side of the tea. For the table centerpiece, consider a lovely holiday floral arrangement with candles at each side.

Tea Servers

Being asked to pour tea is an honor just short of knighthood (as Miss Manners puts it). One week before the event takes place, ask two close friends to help "pour" at the tea. You may encourage them to trade duties each hour during the event. Not only can your friends assist in pouring the tea as you are greeting at the door, they can also be your prayer partners concerning the event. And do pray! This tea is an opportunity to honor the Lord in your home as you share His love with your neighbors and friends. Ask the Lord to bless this occasion and the people who participate.

Arrival

As guests arrive, you should be stationed at the door greeting each visitor with a warm smile and salutation. Assist the guests with their coats, purses, and name tags. Encourage the ladies to make their way to the buffet table where they can have tea or punch and a variety of foods. This is a time of nibbling, chatting, and getting to know one another.

Tea Buffet Menu

Savory Scones
Christmas Wreath Finger Sandwiches
Christmas Cookie Cutter Sandwiches
Raspberry Jam Tarts
Pumpkin Bread with Cream Cheese
Cranberry Coffee Cake
Holiday Almond Fingers

An informal afternoon tea provides midday finger foods and snacks; it is not intended to be an entire meal. Choose your items from the above menu.

Savory Scones

(From the kitchen of Carol Potts)

2 cups self-rising flour	1 Tbsp baking powder
pinch of salt	2 Tbsp cold butter, cut
1–1⅓ cup milk	

❖ Sift together flour, baking powder, and salt in large bowl.
❖ With fingers, rub butter into mixture until crumbly. Make a well in middle of mix, add milk; mix with fork to make a dough that barely holds together. Press dough onto lightly floured surface and knead lightly—just until smooth. Roll dough out and cut out 12 scones using round biscuit or cookie cutter. Put scones on large greased baking sheet. Bake for 8–10 minutes in preheated 450° oven.
❖ DO NOT DOUBLE RECIPE.
❖ Serve with clotted cream, strawberry jam, and lemon curd.
❖ Yields: 12 scones.

Carol adds this interesting scone history: Scones originated in Scotland where the word is pronounced "scaun." The name originally came from a parish in Perthshire, which was the site of the historic abbey and palace where the kings of Scotland were crowned on the Stone of Scone (Destiny). Tradition has said that this stone was Jacob's pillow.

Christmas Wreath Finger Sandwiches

1 (5 oz) jar sharp cheddar cheese food spread	
1 (3 oz) pkg cream cheese, softened	
¼ tsp onion powder	⅛ tsp garlic powder
10 slices white bread	1 cup chopped fresh parsley
sliced pimento	

❖ Combine cheddar cheese, cream cheese, onion and garlic powders, beating until smooth and creamy. Spread on bread slices. Cut bread slices into 2-inch round circles using biscuit or cookie cutter. Cut a small center hole; lightly sprinkle parsley on wreaths and decorate with pimento looped to resemble a bow.
❖ Yields 20 finger sandwiches.

Christmas Cookie Cutter Sandwiches

Your favorite Christmas cookie cutters will help create simple Christmas finger sandwiches on white or wheat bread. Use this delicious chicken-almond filling or thin slices of peeled cucumbers with a spread of cream cheese.

Chicken-Almond Filling
>   2 cups of chopped white meat chicken
>   ½ cup blanched almonds.   2 Tbsp drained crushed pineapple
>   mayonnaise (enough to make a spreadable mixture)

❖ Grind together chicken and almonds. Stir in 2 Tbsp drained crushed pineapple and enough mayonnaise to make a spreadable mixture.
❖ Yields filling for 25–30 finger sandwiches.

Raspberry Jam Tarts

1	(8 oz) cream cheese	2	cups sifted flour
½	lb butter or margarine	1	small jar raspberry jam

❖ Cream butter and cream cheese together. Add flour gradually. Roll in a ball and chill in freezer. Cut in half and roll out very thin. Cut with biscuit or round cookie cutter and add ½ tsp jam. Fold over into triangle, crimp with fork to stick together. Bake on ungreased cookie sheet in 375° oven for 12–15 minutes.
❖ Yields: 24–30 tarts.

Pumpkin Bread with Cream Cheese

½	cup butter or margarine, softened		
1	cup sugar	2	eggs
1¾	cups all-purpose flour	1	tsp baking soda
½	tsp salt	1	tsp ground cinnamon
½	tsp ground nutmeg	¼	tsp ground ginger
¼	tsp ground cloves	1	(15 oz) can pumpkin pie filling

❖ Cream butter, gradually adding sugar. Beat eggs and add to mixture. In separate bowl combine flour, soda, salt, and spices; slowly add to creamed mixture. Gradually add pumpkin pie filling. Pour mixture into well-greased and floured loaf pan. Bake for 1 hour at 350° or until a toothpick inserted in center comes out clean. Cool in pan for 10 minutes; remove from pan and cool on a wire rack. Slice bread and cut each slice in fourths. Make mini-sandwiches using cream cheese as a filling.
❖ Yields approximately 25 sandwiches.

Cranberry Coffeecake

½ cup margarine	1 cup walnut or pecan pieces
1 can whole cranberries	2½ cups white sugar
1 cup brown sugar	1 box yellow cake mix
eggs	oil

❖ Slice margarine into thin slices and arrange evenly in the bottom of a 9 x 13 pan. Sprinkle nuts over the butter. In separate bowl combine white and brown sugar. Add cranberries and toss lightly. Distribute sugared cranberries evenly over nut layer. Prepare yellow cake mix batter according to directions and pour batter over cranberries. Bake at 350° for 40 minutes or until toothpick inserted in the center comes out clean. Cool 10 minutes; loosen edges with a knife and turn pan over on a plate. Slice in small squares and serve with whipped cream.

❖ Yields 12–15 servings.

Holiday Almond Fingers

(This recipe requires real butter, no substitutes, but it's worth it!)

1 cup butter, softened	½ cup powdered sugar
1½ cup all-purpose flour	salt
1 tsp almond extract	2 cups chopped toasted almonds
powdered sugar	

❖ In large bowl cream butter and sugar. Add flour mixed with salt; blend well; beat in almond extract. Stir in almonds; chill about an hour for easier handling. Pinch about a Tbsp of batter and roll between palms of hands into a 2-inch cylinder about ½ inch thick. Place on lightly greased cookie sheets and bake at 325° for 20 minutes or until very lightly browned. Remove cookies to a flat pan onto which you have sifted powdered sugar, then sift more sugar over top of cookies. Freezes well.

❖ Yields approximately 6 dozen.

Tea and Punch

When hosting a tea, use loose tea—avoid tea bags. Follow these helpful tips in preparing tea:

❖ Warm the teapot by rinsing with boiling water.

❖ Use one teaspoonful of loose tea per person, plus "one for the pot."

❖ Bring water to boil (not allowing it to rattle once it boils, as this decreases the oxygen in the water).

❖ Take the teapot to the stove and pour in the boiling water from the kettle. This is important so as to keep the water at boiling point as it is poured over the tea. Ceramic tea pots are best as they retain the heat well.

❖ Generally you will need 1¼ pints of boiling water to each ounce of loose tea.

❖ Stir the tea mixture and replace the lid. Allow the tea to infuse for five minutes. Judge by time, not color, as different teas produce various colors.

❖ Pour tea into warm cups using a strainer to catch leaves. Add sugar to taste. If milk (not cream) is desired, it should be added to the cup before the tea is poured.

Holiday Apple Tea

mellow black tea leaves such as Darjeeling or
　English Breakfast (allow 1 tsp per cup)
clear apple juice　　　　　　cinnamon sticks

❖ Following the traditional method of tea making as you read above; boil apple juice instead of water and pour over black tea leaves. Pour into tea cups, add sugar, and serve with a cinnamon stick.

Christmas Punch

2　(6 oz) cans frozen orange juice
1　(6 oz) can frozen lemonade
1　cup pineapple juice　　　¼　cup cherry juice
2　quarts ginger ale, chilled　　ice

❖ Mix fruit juices; cover and let stand for 12 hours or more in refrigerator. Add cold ginger ale to juices just before serving. Serve over crushed ice or freeze half the ginger ale in ice cube trays.

❖ Yields 24 servings.

Mints and nuts added to the buffet table will make the tea complete.

After-Tea Fellowship

After your guests have had a chance to eat and visit with others, get their attention and thank them for coming to tea. Introduce the "Tea Servers" and thank them for their help.

Lead into a short talk by mentioning that you realize what a busy time of year this is for most people. Ladies especially have a large load as they bake, shop, wrap, decorate, and send cards. Ask your guests if they, too, feel the pressure of the season. Mention that just as there are certain pressures during this time, there are also certain delights. Ask the ladies what are some of their favorite Christmas symbols or decorations at Christmas. In other words, what is the item that they bring down from the attic each December that is most meaningful to them?

Allow several women to respond. Tell the ladies that you have a few items that you want to show them. Show each object (which you will have gathered before the party) and tell of its significance to Christmas.

Symbols of the Season

Candles. Candles add a wonderful glow to the holidays as they are used in advent wreaths, table centerpieces, even small votive bags that line the walkways at Christmas. The candle symbolizes light that illuminates the darkness. The apostle John called Jesus, "The true light which, coming into the world, enlightens every man" (John 1:9, NASB). Jesus came to give us light in a darkened world. Light not only warms and comforts but it also reveals. This Christmas season, may you come to know the Light of the world whom we celebrate.

Candy Canes. These sweet treats that we see so often during this season portray a beautiful message as well. The bent shape of the candy reminds us of a shepherd's crook. Jesus called Himself the Good Shepherd, who cares for His sheep. Jesus knows and cares for us. (If you turn the shepherd's crook upside down you see a *J* standing for Jesus.) The red and white stripes remind us of the purity of Jesus' life intertwined with the blood that He shed when He died on the cross for us. Isaiah 53:5, referring to Christ's suffering for us, says that "by His stripes we are healed."

Christmas Tree. As I look at the evergreen I see the shape of an arrow pointing up to God. This is how our lives should be, pointing to God and focusing on Him. The evergreen itself reminds me of eternal life. Green is a living color; it represents living things. What a perfect tree to use at Christmas as we celebrate the birth of Jesus who brings us eternal life. It is only through trusting Him that we ourselves can be "evergreen" as it says in John 3:16 (TLB): "For God loved the world so much that he gave his only Son so that anyone who believes in Him shall not perish but have eternal life."

Favorite Christmas Dishes. Many of us enjoy the wonderful food during the holiday season. But have you noticed that even after you have eaten a wonderful meal, the next day you are hungry all over again? Food provides temporary satisfaction to ease the stomach hunger and bless the palate. Jesus said, "I am the bread of life. He who comes to Me shall never hunger, and he who believes in Me shall never thirst" (John 6:35). We each hunger spiritually to know God and be forgiven of our sins. Jesus satisfies that hunger, and we will never hunger again. Read John 6:48–51.

Christmas Music or Bells. I love the wonderful music at Christmastime—the carols and the instrumentals. As I listen to the glorious music, it reminds me of one of the greatest concerts of all time to a most unlikely audience. As shepherds were keeping their flocks one night, an angel appeared to them announcing the birth of a savior, Christ the Lord. The angels broke out in a heavenly concert that night. What a glorious experience it must have been! One day I hope to hear a repeat performance of that concert. The Bible says that those who believe in Jesus will one day be with Him in heaven (John 14:1–6).

Angels. Angels are quite popular today, and it is important to understand who they are and what they do. In the Bible they have several functions. Some angels serve as messengers (Luke 1:26–31), others proclaim God's holiness (Isa. 6:2–5), others act as God's soldiers carrying out judgment, making war, or protecting God's people (2 Kings 19:35; Matt. 18:10, Rev. 12:7). Angels get their power from God. We pray to God and not to angels. They are God's helpers, and they remind us of God's special care for us.

Tree Ornaments. Beautiful, reflective, symbolic, yet fragile. Ornaments remind me of the fragile state of man and the brevity of life. Yet as each glass ornament shines, it reminds me of how Jesus told us to shine for Him (Matt. 5:16). As the ornaments glorify the tree, so should we glorify the Father with our lives.

Crèche Or Manger Scene. Not only does the manger scene keep our focus on the true meaning of the season, it reminds us of the lowly state in which God chose to give His Son to the world. Jesus could have arrived in a palace with great riches, yet God chose a dirty, smelly animal stable, with the baby Jesus placed in a feeding trough. How humble! How beautiful! God wanted us to see that Jesus was human as we are and could relate to the most humble among us. I'm so thankful that we have a God to whom we can relate, who chose to humble Himself to show his love for us.

Presents, Gifts, Packages. Isn't it interesting that God's greatest gift came in ordinary wrapping—a precious baby, a real person, a normal human being. Yet this present contains the most incredible gift. The Bible says that there is no greater love than to give your life for a friend (John 15:13). That's what Jesus did for us. He willingly gave His life on the cross, providing eternal life and forgiveness of sins for those who believe. There is even more to the package, as He provides help in daily living through the Holy Spirit and His Word. Thanks be to God for His unspeakable Gift!

As you close, tell the ladies that God's wonderful gift is available to all who choose to believe. Read Acts 16:31: "Believe on the Lord Jesus Christ, and you will be saved." Encourage your guests to read the Gospel of John during this holiday season. Close in prayer.

Allow time for mingling and questions at the end of the presentation. Some of your guests may want to ask you about a local church or Bible study program. Others may want to know about special Christmas programs or Christmas Eve services. Be prepared to answer their questions with helpful information about local events and churches (not necessarily your own).

Tea Favors

Perhaps you would like to give a little gift to your guests as they leave. Attach small cards with Scripture to accompany the gift items. Gift ideas include:

- A copy of a favorite poem either framed, decorated, or laminated.
- A small loaf of bread or bundle of tea cookies.
- A handmade craft item.
- A special teacup or mug.
- A small box of tea or a jar of homemade jam.
- An explanation of the advent wreath and several candles.
- A Christmas tree ornament, store-bought or homemade.
- A small basket or box containing cards with special verses, sayings and poems.

Final Note

A word of encouragement to the hostess: Most people long to have a meaningful Christmas holiday and to understand more of Christ's significance in their lives. This tea is the perfect occasion to present Christ in a very real and practical way. Be sincere, honest, and careful not to overuse "Christian dialogue."

There are a variety of ways to share God's love at this Christmas gathering. Other ideas include asking someone special to come and give a brief Christmas message. Or perhaps you would like to read a story or poem that portrays God's wonderful love and gift of salvation. Ask God's direction as to how best to relate His message to your guests.

Let the redeemed of the LORD say so.

PSALM 107:2

Chapter 22

Low Maintenance

HOLIDAY PROGRESSIVE DINNER

PROGRESSIVE SCHEDULE		
30 Minutes	House #1 •	Greetings and appetizers
30 Minutes	House #2 •	Soup and salad
60 Minutes	House #3 •	Main course
60 Minutes	House #4 •	Dessert, coffee, game (game optional)

'Tis the season to go to Christmas parties! This year why not try something different? How about a Christmas progressive dinner? Visit four houses, each serving a course of a delicious meal. After organizing the houses, your preparation for this party will be fairly easy. Enjoy this holiday extravaganza with all of the guests, and who knows, this may become an annual event!

Old-Time Map Invitations

Create an old world map to use as the invitation and directions to the progressive dinner. Print the invitations on parchment paper and burn the edges to make it look old. The information should read as follows:

As wise men followed the star
to Bethlehem many years ago,
We follow this map; the route
to a Progressive Dinner it will show.

Join your friends at _____ o'clock
to start the evening along.
At ___: ___ the evening will end
with dessert and joyful song.

We look forward to seeing you
on (day) the (date) of December.
(phone number) is the RSVP
number to remember!

Draw a map showing all of the houses involved in the progressive dinner. Clearly number each house in the order it will be visited. Write a key on the side of the map with the house number, address, and phone number.

You will need to estimate the time for your progressive dinner, taking into consideration the driving time to each house. Generally the first and second courses will take about thirty minutes, while the main course and dessert/games will be about an hour each.

Progressive Dinner Instructions

How to Choose the Homes

In choosing the host homes for the different phases of the dinner, you will need to first consider location. If you live in a big city, you do not want your guests spending the majority of the evening driving for miles to each location. Keep the party in one area of town if possible. You will also need to consider who can handle the various courses of the dinner. You will need a bigger home with tables and chairs available for the main course.

How do you ask someone if they will help host the progressive dinner? Ask only people who would naturally be invited to the dinner anyway. Simply say, "I am in the process of planning a progressive dinner for our _____ group. Would you be interested in opening your home to host the _____ course of the dinner?"

Progressive dinners are a wonderful opportunity to encourage people to practice hospitality. This may be the catalyst that some people need to help them see that entertaining others can be a blessing! People who cannot host the event in their home may help by preparing food for the dinner and dropping it off at the designated home on the day of the party.

Creative Variations

You could make this party a "Christmas Around the World" Progressive Dinner. At each home, experience food from a different country and learn of their unique Christmas customs. Your local library will be a good source of help for food recipes and information on international holiday celebrations. Each home can be decorated according to the country it is representing.

Another idea is to focus on the various Christmas carols of the season and the stories that go with each one. At each house tell the story behind a Christmas carol and lead everyone in the singing of that carol. Decorations and invitations can center around musical notes, instruments, and sheet music.

Christmas Story Decorations

Host homes for the progressive dinner will most likely be decorated with their own Christmas decorations. A wonderful way to add a theme to the decorations is to allow each home to focus on one aspect of the Christmas story, progressively leading to Jesus in the manger. At the first house center on

Gabriel's announcement to Mary using angel figures in the yard and throughout the house. Add trumpets and harps and play soft harp music in the background.

The second house will center their decorations around the shepherds on the hillside. Wooden sheep made from plywood, painted or covered with cotton or wool, make a nice display in the yard. Shepherd and sheep figurines and shepherds' staffs can enhance the Christmas decorations inside. For background music, play Christmas carols sung by a boys' choir.

The third house will incorporate the entire stable scene. Figures of Mary, Joseph, and the baby Jesus will be the decorations both in the yard and house. Use Christmas carols sung by choirs or popular Christian artists as background music. The fourth and final house will focus on the star and wisemen. Camels, crowns, stars, and decorated gold boxes representing the gifts will all make wonderful decorations. Play majestic music, perhaps Handel's *Messiah* in the background.

At the first home you will need to offer name tags to your guests. The name tags can be in the form of a star or simply use holiday tags. You will also need to have extra maps available at the first house in case someone has forgotten theirs.

Each home can choose their own dinnerware for serving. At the home for appetizers, plastic or paper holiday plates and cups are appropriate. For the salad course, the hostess may choose whether to serve buffet-style or sit down at tables. Either way is fine and she may choose china or plastic according to what she has available. At the main course house, it would be nice to offer a sit-down dinner using china or Christmas plates if possible. The dessert house can again be more casual, using paper or plastic goods with dessert and coffee served buffet-style.

Progressive Holiday Menu

Appetizers • House #1

Christmas Cranberry Wassail
Shrimp Dip
Party Sausage Balls
Hearty Artichoke Squares
Bacon and Pecan Cheese Log
Raw Vegetables with Dill Dip

Christmas Cranberry Wassail

2½	cups boiling water	6	tea bags
¼	tsp cinnamon	¼	tsp nutmeg
¼	tsp allspice	¾	cup sugar
½	cup orange juice	⅓	cup lemon juice
1 ½	cups water	1	pint cranberry juice cocktail

❖ Steep tea bags and spices in boiling water for 5 minutes. Strain tea and stir in sugar until dissolved. Add rest of the ingredients and serve either hot or cold.
❖ I suggest making several batches at a time.
❖ Yields 10–12 servings.

Shrimp Dip

From the kitchen of Susan Hill.

1	(8 oz) pkg cream cheese
½	lb fresh chopped shrimp (already cooked)
1	stick butter　　1　Tbsp chives
	dash of cayenne pepper

❖ Melt cream cheese and butter in saucepan; add shrimp and spices. Stir until heated throughout. Serve with variety of crackers.

Party Sausage Balls

2	cups biscuit mix	1	lb sausage (uncooked)
1	cup grated cheddar cheese		

❖ Blend all ingredients. Make small balls (about ½ tsp each). Bake 250° for 20–25 minutes until done. Serve hot.
❖ Yields approximately 3 dozen balls.

Hearty Artichoke Squares

1 (6 oz) jar marinated artichoke hearts
1 (14 oz) can plain artichoke hearts, drained
1 small onion, finely chopped
1 clove garlic, minced   4 eggs
¼ cup fine bread crumbs   2 tsp parsley, minced
¼ tsp salt   ⅛ tsp oregano
¼ tsp Tabasco
½ lb sharp cheddar cheese, shredded

❖ Drain marinade from jar of artichokes, reserving juice.
  Chop all artichokes. Sauté onion and garlic in marinade
  juice. Beat eggs and add crumbs and seasonings. Stir in
  cheese, parsley, artichokes, and onion mixture. Turn into a
  greased 6 x 10 baking pan. Bake at 325° for 30 minutes.
  Allow to cool in pan. Cut into 1-inch squares. Serve hot or
  cold. Freezes well.
❖ Yields 60 squares.

Bacon and Pecan Cheese Log

1 lb bacon
1 (8 oz) pkg cream cheese, softened
½ cup chopped pecans   ¼ tsp garlic salt
¼ tsp Worcestershire sauce   4 drops hot pepper sauce
1 Tbsp chili powder

❖ Cook bacon until crisp; drain and crumble. Blend with
  remaining ingredients except chili powder. Shape into 2
  rolls about 1 inch in diameter. Sprinkle chili powder to coat
  evenly. Wrap tightly in waxed paper. Chill. Slice and serve
  on or with crackers.
❖ Yields about 5 dozen servings.

Raw Vegetables with Dill Dip

❖ Arrange carrot sticks, celery curls, sliced zucchini, broccoli
  florets, radishes, and mushrooms on a plate.
❖ Place a bowl of Dill Dip in the center of the plate.

Combine the following Dill Dip ingredients:

1 cup mayonnaise   2 cups sour cream
2 Tbsp dillweed   1 Tbsp minced parsley
   dash of salt

Soup and Salad • House #2

Caesar Salad with Homemade Croutons
Creamy Tomato Curry Soup
Cheese Wafers

Caesar Salad

 1 cup grated Parmesan cheese
 ¼ cup lemon juice
 1 large clove garlic, peeled and crushed
 1 egg   2 tsp Worcestershire sauce
 ½ cup olive oil   2 large heads of romaine lettuce
   salt and pepper to taste

❖ Combine garlic, lemon juice, egg, Worcestershire sauce, salt, and pepper in blender. Process 6–8 seconds or until well blended. Keep blender running as oil is slowly added. Tear lettuce into bite-size pieces, wash thoroughly, dry, and place in salad bowl. Refrigerate until ready to serve. Add cheese to salad and top with homemade croutons. Pour dressing over salad and toss gently just before serving.

❖ Yields 12–15 servings.

Homemade Croutons

 4 slices dry homestyle white bread
 3 Tbsp olive oil   1 large clove garlic, minced

❖ Trim crusts from bread and cut bread into ½-inch cubes. Arrange cubes in single layer on baking sheet and toast at 300° until crisp (about 15 minutes). Remove cubes from oven and set aside. Line large plate with paper towels. In medium-sized skillet heat oil over medium heat. Add garlic and bread cubes and sauté, constantly stirring and turning the cubes for 5–7 minutes or until cubes are golden. Transfer croutons to paper towel-lined plate to drain.

Creamy Tomato Curry Soup

 6 cups tomato juice   4 Tbsp tomato paste
 8 scallions, minced   salt
   pinch of powdered thyme   ½ tsp curry powder
   freshly ground pepper   2 Tbsp lemon juice
 1 cup sour cream   chopped parsley

❖ Combine and heat all ingredients (except sour cream and parsley) over medium heat. Just before serving, stir in sour cream, blending well. Garnish with parsley. Serve with cheese wafers.

❖ Yields 12 servings.

Cheese Wafers

1 stick butter	5 oz grated sharp cheddar cheese
⅛ tsp cayenne pepper	½ tsp salt
1 cup flour	¼ tsp Worcestershire sauce

❖ Soften butter and grated cheese to room temperature; mix together. Mix dry ingredients and Worcestershire sauce and roll into marble-sized balls. Place on ungreased cookie sheet and mash each ball down with a teaspoon. Bake at 275° for 35–40 minutes.

❖ Yields 24 wafers.

Water, soft drinks, or apple cider are possible beverages.

Main Course • House #3

> *Baked Ham with Applesauce Glaze*
> *Spinach Casserole*
> *Twice-Baked Potatoes*
> *Dinner Rolls*

Baked Ham with Applesauce Glaze

Place whole ham fat-side up on rack in open roasting pan. Cover with foil. Bake at 325°, 18–20 minutes per pound. Meat thermometer should read internal temperature of 160°. During the last 30 minutes of baking, score fat in diamond shapes; stick a whole clove in each diamond and pour ¾ cup of glaze (recipe below) over ham. Heat the remaining sauce and serve with ham.

Glaze: Combine all ingredients.

¼ cup brown sugar	½ cup honey
1 cup applesauce	1 tsp dry mustard

❖ You may want to substitute this baked ham with a store-bought, spiral cut, or honey-glazed baked ham.

Spinach Casserole

8 slices bacon, cooked until crisp, drained
2 (10 oz) pkgs frozen chopped spinach, cooked and drained

2 eggs	1 cup milk
1 tsp salt	⅔ cup bread crumbs
4 tsp minced onion	1½ cup grated cheddar cheese
paprika	

❖ Beat eggs with milk and salt. Add spinach, crumbled bacon, bread crumbs, onion, and ¾ cup cheese. Pour into greased 1½ quart casserole dish. Sprinkle with additional cheese and paprika. Bake uncovered at 350° for 25–30 minutes.
❖ Yields 8–10 servings.

Twice-Baked Potatoes

5 medium potatoes	½ pint sour cream
½ cup milk	5 strips crisp bacon, crumbled
1 large onion, chopped	1 Tbsp chives, chopped
1 tsp minced garlic	3 Tbsp grated cheddar cheese

❖ Bake potatoes. Scoop potato from shell. Mash with sour cream and milk. Mix in bacon, onion, chives, and seasoning. Fill shell halves and top with cheese. Bake at 325° for 30 minutes.
❖ Yields 10 servings.

Serve your favorite dinner rolls or bread along with this wonderful main course, with tea and/or water as beverages.

Desserts • House #4

Yule Log Cake
Individual Pecan Tarts
Cran-Apple Bake

Choose one of the following desserts or provide all three for a special variety!

Yule Log Cake

5 eggs, separated	1 cup powdered sugar
3 Tbsp cocoa	chocolate frosting (canned is fine)
2 cups whipped cream	¾ cup chopped walnuts

❖ Beat egg yolks until thick and pale. Add powdered sugar and cocoa and beat well again. Beat egg whites until stiff, fold into yolk mixture. Spread batter evenly in a large buttered and floured 15½ x 10½ x 1 jellyroll pan. Bake at 350° for 12–15 minutes, until knife inserted comes out clean. Quickly turn cake out onto a damp towel sprinkled with additional powdered sugar. Roll the cake in the towel and cool.

❖ Unroll the cake. Spread it very lightly with 3 Tbsp chocolate frosting and thickly with 2 cups whipped cream. Roll again. Spread chocolate frosting over the roll using a spatula to make a rough surface. Decorate with swirls of frosting from pastry tube. Sprinkle the ends of log with chopped walnuts. Refrigerate and slice when ready to serve.

Individual Pecan Tarts

Pastry:
    1 (3 oz) pkg cream cheese   ½ cup butter, softened
    1 cup all-purpose flour

Filling:
    3 Tbsp melted butter   ¾ cup firmly packed dark brown sugar
    2 eggs, slightly beaten   1 cup chopped pecans

❖ Combine cream cheese, butter, and flour together until smooth. Lightly grease and flour 10 muffin cups and pat mixture into tins, leaving the center of each tart hollow. Combine filling ingredients and spoon into center of each tart. Bake at 350° for 25 minutes. Cool before removing from tins.

❖ Yields 10 tarts.

Cran-Apple Bake

    3 cups tart apples, peeled and diced
    2 cups fresh whole cranberries
    1 cup granulated sugar   1 cup chopped pecans
    ½ cup brown sugar   ⅓ cup flour
    1½ cups rolled oats   ½ cup melted butter

❖ Mix apples, cranberries, and 1 cup sugar and put in 10 x 13 pan. Mix rest of ingredients and sprinkle over fruit. Bake 1 hour at 325°. Serve with ice cream or whipped cream.

❖ Yields 12–15 servings.

Serve both regular and decaf coffee with a variety of creams, sugars, and toppings.

Party Activities

For Every House

At each house read the portion of the Christmas story that is represented by the decorations. Here are the passages of Scripture to be read at each home:

> House #1: Luke 1:26–37 (Angel Gabriel talks to Mary)
> House #2: Luke 2:8–20 (Story of shepherds)
> House #3: Luke 2:1–7 (Jesus born in a stable)
> House #4: Matthew 2:1–11 (Visit of the wise men)

The host or hostess at the location should offer a prayer of thanks for God's wonderful gift of Jesus.

For after Dinner (House #4)

At the final home you may want to play a game or activity after dinner. Here are a few ideas from which to choose.

Christmas Carols. Sing favorite Christmas carols together as a group. If one of your guests plays the guitar or piano, ask him to accompany the group or use a tape. Do some research from the library to find the history of some favorite Christmas carols and share the information in the form of trivia questions to the group between songs. Consider caroling door to door in the neighborhood.

Light a Candle, Give a Gift. Give each guest a candle. Dim the lights and light one candle. Ask each guest to consider one gift they can give from the heart to their family or friends this Christmas. The person with the lighted candle states their gift then lights the candle next to theirs. The light is passed on until every candle is lit and everyone has told of their gift from the heart this season. Gift ideas include: Call Grandma once a week, do the laundry without grumbling, write a note of encouragement to friends on a regular basis, serve the community in a specific way this year. Close this activity by reading Matthew 5:16. Jesus called His disciples "the light of the world" and said, "Let your light so shine before men, that they may see your good works and glorify your Father in heaven."

Trim the Tree. Give each guest a 1-foot square of aluminum foil and a ribbon. Allow three minutes for the contest. Each person is to shape the foil into a meaningful ornament for the Christmas tree. After three minutes, ask each person to show their ornament to the group and tell about its meaning. The group will then vote on the best ornament as well as other awards, such as most symbolic ornament, most artistic, and most unique or original. Use the ribbons to hang the ornaments on the tree. Put a number on each ornament. Allow guests to draw numbers from a basket before they leave. They will take the correlating ornament home as a reminder of the event.

Grab Bag Gift Exchange. On the invitation ask each guest to bring a small wrapped gift under five dollars in value. Place all of the gifts in a large pillowcase. Put numbers on slips of paper and let each person draw a number. Going in numerical order, let the first person pick a gift from the bag. This person opens the gift for all to see. The next person then chooses a gift. Before she opens it she must decide if she wants to keep it or trade for the first person's gift. Play continues as each person has the option to open his gift or trade the unopened gift for one that a previous player has opened.

Wrap for the Needy Assembly Line. Include in the invitation that everyone should bring an unwrapped toy to be donated to a needy family or organization. Let everyone participate in the wrapping of the gifts by setting up an assembly line. The first person in line will write a description card saying to whom the present should go. The following person will cut a sheet of wrapping paper. The next few people will tape one side of the wrapping paper around the package. The next person will place bows on the package, while the last person will attach the card.

This will be a fun activity in which everyone can participate. Start two assembly lines if you have enough people. If you have time and it is not too late, take the gifts to the recipients after the wrapping. You may want to prepare several food baskets in assembly line manner as well.

My Favorite Christmas Memories. Allow each person to write their favorite Christmas memory on an index card. Gather the cards and read them one at a time without telling who the person is. Ask everyone to make a guess as to who they think wrote the Christmas memory and then reveal the true author. This is a delightful way to get to know a little more about each other.

Gifts or Favors

If you would like to hand your guests a small gift from this memorable evening, consider the following suggestions:

- Tree ornament, homemade or store-bought
- Small decorated gold box with Scripture or plan of salvation written on a card inside
- Small bag of Christmas cookies or other home-baked items
- Hot chocolate mix and a mug
- Small plastic frame decorated with Christmas stickers or ribbons

Final Note

Christmas is the time of the year that should bring us joy, but many times it brings us stress and frustration. We are too busy to do a puzzle with the kids or chat with a friend because we must shop, bake, write, wrap, and prepare for the holidays. I'm reminded again of Jesus' words, "Martha, Martha, you are worried and troubled about many things. But one thing is needed, and Mary has chosen that good part, which will not be taken away from her" (Luke 10:41–42).

What cares are you worried and bothered about this season? What is truly necessary? What can wait? Perhaps only a few things are necessary, really only one.

> "For there is born to you this day in the city of David a Savior who is Christ the Lord."
>
> LUKE 2:11

CONCLUSION

Ready to host a party? Once you have planned, prepared, and invited your guests, remember one more important aspect of your preparations—prayer. I'm not just referring to the "grace" that is said before dinner (although that is important); I am talking about asking the Lord's blessing on the entire event before it actually takes place.

Commit the party to God and ask that He would be glorified in your home. Ask the Lord to bless the people who attend the party and their conversations. Prayer prepares our hearts and minds to serve our guests in a gracious and loving manner. As you pray you will find your attention will be drawn away from yourself and the perfections of the party, and your focus will be placed on One who deserves the honor.

First Corinthians 10:31 says, "Therefore, whether you eat or drink, or whatever you do, do all to the glory of God." Honor Christ in your home by showing His love and hospitality to all who enter. May you build many happy memories and meaningful relationships through simple and creative parties!

RECIPE INDEX

Desserts

Main Dishes

Vegetables and Side Dishes

ACTIVITIES INDEX